MW01641593

I Am HER

Healing* Evolving* Rising

A Spiritual and Practical Guide for Black Women Ready to Stop Surviving and Start Rising

AUTHOR
Donita Stansell

I am HER

Healing* Evolving* Rising

Dedication

To the women who came before me. To the grandmothers who held worlds together with tired hands and unbent spines. To the mothers who stretched paychecks, meals, and mercy until they covered everybody but themselves. To the aunties, big cousins, play mamas, church mothers, and neighborhood sheroes who raised whole communities on borrowed strength. To the Black women who swallowed their own tears so we could laugh louder. To the ones who took the jobs nobody wanted, rode the buses that wouldn't welcome them, worked the shifts that stole their sleep, stayed in places they should've been able to leave—all while praying that the next generation would have it better.

To the women whose names I know and to the ancestors whose names I will never know, but whose blood, courage, and whispers live in my bones... This is for you. For every time you wanted to rest but kept going. For every dream you laid down so your children could pick theirs up. For every "I'm fine" you said when you were anything but. For every boundary you weren't allowed to have, for every "no" you never got to say, for every "yes" you gave that cost you more than it should have. I honor your survival. I honor your sacrifice. I honor your faith.

And with this book, I make you a quiet promise I will not let your suffering be the only story we inherit. I will heal where you were not given the tools to heal. I will evolve in places you were forced to stay the same. I will rise in rooms you were never allowed to enter—not just for me, but for the daughters and sons who come after me. I pray that as I Heal, Evolve, and Rise, I am living out the answered prayers you sent up on nights nobody saw.

This book is my love letter, my thank you, and my declaration because of you, I am HER.

And, because I am HER, the women who come after me won't have to start where I started.

For all the women before me—this is your flower, in my words. For my mother, Janice P. Ingram-Webster, my grandmother, Bessie Mae Gunnels-Ingram, my God-Mother Linda McMurray-Williams, and in loving memory of my sister, Latricia Banks, whose lives planted the seeds of this book. Lastly, to every Black Woman reading this, you are the continuation of a miracle!

Introduction

Dear HER,

You! My Sister with the tired eyes and the fierce spirit. The one everyone calls strong. The one they call for advice, prayer, money, rides, babysitting, ideas, and emotional support. The one who holds it all together when it feels like everything is falling apart. This is for you.

I do not know exactly where you are as you read this. Maybe you are sitting in your car in the driveway, taking five breaths before you go into the house. Maybe you are on your lunch break at a job that pays you but does not really see you. Maybe the kids are finally asleep. Maybe your heart is broken. Maybe you are in a good place on paper, but your soul is whispering, "There has to be more than this"! Wherever you are, I wrote this book with you in mind. I wrote it for the woman who loves God but sometimes wonders if He sees how much she is carrying. For the woman who smiles in the group photo but cries in the shower. For the woman who is grateful for her life but also exhausted by the version of herself she had to become just to survive.

I wrote this for the girl inside you who was told to be strong before she was ever allowed to just be soft. People see your crown, but they do not always see the weight. They see your results, but not the tears you cried to get there. They see your confidence, but not the doubt you wrestled with in the dark. I see you. And more importantly, God sees you.

This book is not here to tell you to "be stronger" or "do more." this is not another "fix yourself" project. This book is an invitation. A pause. A mirror. A conversation between you, me, God, and every Black woman who has ever felt like she had to hold the whole world in her hands. We are going on a journey together.

A HER journey. *HEALING. EVOLVING. RISING.* We start with HEAL, because before you can evolve or rise, you must tell the truth about the wounds. About the pressure. About the moments you felt unseen, unheard, and unprotected. Healing is not weakness. Healing is you returning to yourself. It is you saying, "I deserve to feel whole, not just functional."

Then we EVOLVE. That is where we go from survival mode to intentional living. From people-pleasing to purpose-led choices. From "I am just happy to be here" to "I belong here." It is the part where you start aligning your mindset, your boundaries, your relationships, and your moves with who you really are, not who the world trained you to be.

And then, sis, we RISE. Not in a fake, performative, "look at me" way. But in a grounded, God-backed way. Rise as in owning your voice at work. Asking what you are worth, the compensation for what you deserve. Building legacy. Leading from a place of wholeness. Designing a life that feels like truth, not obligation. Each chapter in this book will meet you in two places at once, your spirit and your everyday life. You will find stories and real talk that remind you are not alone, spiritual reflections, prayers, or affirmations that help you reconnect with God and yourself along with practical HER Practices, so you are not just inspired, you are shifting how you think, respond and live.

This is a workbook for your soul and your schedule. For your heart and your hustle. For your calling and your calendar. I am not writing to you as a woman who has it all perfect. I am writing to you as a wife, a mother, grandmother, an entrepreneur, a speaker, a life coach, and a Black woman who has had to unlearn a whole lot of survival just to taste freedom. I am still **Healing**. Still **Evolving**. Still **Rising**. We are in this together. So, as you read, I want you to give yourself permission to underline and highlight, to journal and cry, to pause and pray, lastly, to come back to chapters when life gets loud again.

But, most of all, I want you to give yourself permission to be honest. Dig deep, honest about the weight, honest about the dreams, honest about the fears, honest about the woman you know deep down you are called to be. In this moment we have together, I want you to tap into the expectations you have had to live up to - if all you ever heard was "be strong," let this book be the first time you are told, it's ok to let the wall down and "be held,". Held by God. Held by truth. Held by your own compassion for yourself.

You are HER. Even on the days you do not feel like it. Even on the days you forget. Even on the days you fall back into old patterns. Every page is simply an invitation to come home to yourself again. So, take a deep breath. unclench your jaw. drop your shoulders. This is your space. Your time. Your turn. Let us Heal. Let us Evolve. Let us Rise. Together.

With love, fire, and full belief in you,
Your Sister, Your Friend
Donita

Table of Contents

PART 1
HEALING
Mending What The World Tried To Break

CHAPTER 1

THE WEIGHT SHE CARRIES, THE CROWN SHE WEARS

She sat in her car in the driveway, engine off, keys still in her hand. The porch light was on. Inside, the house was waiting. Kids' homework. Dinner dishes. Text messages from people asking, "You got a minute" Work emails still unread. A voicemail from her mama. A group chat pinging about somebody else's crisis.

On the outside, everybody would say she was doing well. Good job. Good woman. Good wife. Good mother. Good friend. Good church member. She was the one people introduced with pride. "Oh, you gotta meet her. She is amazing. She does it all."

But in that car, in that quiet, she felt the truth settle on her chest. "I am tired." Not the kind of tired a nap will fix. The kind of tired that sits in your bones. The kind of tired that comes from holding it all for a long time, without putting anything down.

Sis, that woman has been me! Reflect on the moments! Maybe you have had your own car moment. Maybe it is the bathroom at work. Maybe it is the shower. Maybe it is that pause in your bed before your feet hit the floor and you slide into performance mode. The world sees your crown. The world sees your cape. But you know in your heart, there is a weight you have been carrying so long you almost forgot it was there. The Weight She Carries, the weight you carry. Let us tell the truth. There is the weight of being the "strong Black woman."

The one who can handle it. The one who does not break. The one who prays for everybody, answers the late-night calls, shows up early, stays late. The one who gets it done without asking for help. The dependable one. The solid one.

There is the weight of being excellent at work but still overlooked. The weight of smiling through microaggressions. Being called "intimidating" when you are just being clear. Being praised in private but passed over in public. Training the new hire who ends up getting the title you deserved.

There is the weight of family expectations. Being the backbone. The mediator. The fixer. The one who sends money. The one who keeps the peace. The one who remembers birthdays. The one who is always "okay" because everyone has gotten used to you not needing anything.

There is the weight of faith and church. Serving on teams. Showing up when you are empty. Being asked to pour out when nobody stops to ask, "Who pours into you"?

And then there is the weight nobody sees. The childhood wounds. The losses you never fully grieved. The secrets you kept to protect people who never protected you. The fear that if you finally say, "I cannot do this," everything and everyone will fall apart. Sis, it's a lot, I feel you.

Some of us have been carrying so many roles for so long that if somebody asked, "Who are you without all of this" we would not know how to answer.

The Crown She Wears, But here is the part we cannot skip. Yes, there is weight. But there is also a crown. You were not born into this world as a beast of burden. You were born as a masterpiece. A daughter. A reflection of God's glory. A continuation of your mothers and grandmothers' prayers. A walking answer to cries they sent up they never got to see fulfilled.

People see your crown when they say things like, "You are so strong," or "You are so smart," or "You always know what to do." They see flashes of your brilliance, your resilience, your beauty, your intelligence, your creativity, your heart. What they do not always see is the cost.

They do not see the late nights. The internal battles. The tears. The moments you almost gave up. The times you questioned yourself. The times you wondered, "Who would I be if I was not always holding everything for everybody" I want you to know something right here at the start of this book.

Your crown is not a reward for suffering. Your crown is not a prize you earned by enduring more than most. Your crown is not the world patting you on the head saying, "Good girl. You survived." Your crown is your birthright.

You came here crowned. You came here worthy. You came here loved. Long before a job title, a relationship status, a bank account, or a degree, you were already valuable. The problem is not that you have a crown. The problem is that somewhere along the way, the world tried to stack its weight on top of it.

When The Crown And The Weight Collide-This is where so many Black women live, every single day. Crowned, yes. Called, yes. Chosen, yes. But, also tired. Also stretched. Also unseen in certain spaces. Also expected to be everything to everybody.

You are expected to be strong, but not "too strong." Soft, but not "too soft." Smart, but not "too opinionated." Present, but not "too demanding."

At work, you may feel like you have to shrink your brilliance just to make other people comfortable. You prepare twice as hard so you can make half the mistakes. You code switch, you edit your words, you second guess your tone in that email.

At home, you might be the organizer, the planner, the counselor, the cook, the driver, the human emotional support, and the glue that holds everybody together. In church or community, you might be the volunteer, the intercessor, the greeter, the one who always says yes. You are "such a blessing" to everyone, while privately feeling depleted.

Sis, the crown, and the weight start to collide, I feel you! You know you are called. You know there is greatness in you. But you are also wondering, "Is this what God meant My whole life in service to everyone else, while I slowly disappear"? You Were Never Created Just To Carry. Let me say this plain. You were not created just to carry. You were not created just to carry burdens, carry people, carry secrets, carry pain, carry everybody's expectations while abandoning your own needs. Yes, God trusted you with strength. Yes, God gave you resilience. Yes, your ancestors passed down a survival that is nothing short of miraculous. But surviving is not the end of your story.

God did not put you here to be everybody's mule. God did not design you to be the one who never rests, never receives, never gets to be held. Even Jesus rested. Even Jesus said no. Even Jesus stepped away from the crowd. Even Jesus slept in the middle of storms. If the Son of God could put some things down and let God be God, what makes you think you are failing if you do the same? Sis, healing starts the moment you allow yourself to believe this simple truth. You are allowed to put some of this weight down.

The Beginning Of HEALING

This first part of the book, HEALING, is not about fixing a broken woman. I do not believe you are beyond repair. I do not believe you are some project. HEAL is about telling the truth. Telling the truth about what it has cost you to wear that "strong Black woman" label. Telling the truth about the nights you cried after being disrespected at work.

Telling the truth about how it felt to be overlooked, underestimated, or overused. Telling the truth about the times you betrayed yourself just to keep the peace. Healing begins when you stop gaslighting your own soul. When you stop saying, "It is not that bad," when you know it is heavy. When you stop pretending that constant exhaustion is "normal."

In this chapter and the ones that follow in HEAL, we are going to:

- Name the weight.
- Unlearn survival that has expired.
- Challenge the lies you have carried in your mind.
- Reconnect with God's vision of you.

We are not rushing. We are not performing. We are not trying to impress anybody. We are simply letting you be honest, maybe for the first time in a long time.

A Softer Look At Yourself

Before we go into the practice for this chapter, I want you to try something.

Imagine a younger version of you. Maybe she is 8. Maybe she is 15. Maybe she is 21. See her in your mind. See her with her big dreams and unfiltered laugh. See the way her eyes shine when she talks about her future.

Now imagine loading that girl up with everything you are carrying right now. All the responsibility. All the pressure. All the perfection. All the expectations. All the secrets. All the "be strong." All the "do not cry." All the "you better not mess this up." Sis, Would you do that to her? Would you look her in the eyes and say, "Here, hold all of this. Never drop it. Never rest. Never fall apart. Never ask for help." You know good and well, of course you would not! So why is it okay when it is you?

Part of healing is starting to look at yourself with the same compassion you have for everyone else. To see the woman in the mirror as worthy of care, not just capable of work. You have carried a lot. But you do not have to carry it all, all the time, all by yourself. Let us begin to gently put some of it down.

HER PRACTICE – *Chapter 1*

The Weight She Carries, The Crown She Wears

HER Reflection: Grab your journal, notes app, or a piece of paper and answer these honestly. No editing. No "shoulds." Just truth.

1. Where in your life do you feel the heaviest right now? Write it out. Describe what that weight feels like:
   - Work
   - Home
   - Church or community
   - Relationships
   - Finances

2. Who trained you to be "the strong one? Think of people, moments, or messages.
   - Did you hear, "Stop crying," "You better not be weak," "You know better," growing up
   - Who did you watch carrying everything

3. When was the last time you let yourself fully rest without guilt?
   - What happened
   - How did it feel
   - How long did it last

4. What are you afraid might happen if you stopped carrying so much? Sis, this is your moment, let it all come out. Be

real!

- "People will be disappointed."
- "Things will fall apart."
- "They will not need me."
- "I will have to feel things I have been avoiding."

HER *Prayer*

You can pray this out loud or in your heart. "God, I bring You the weight I have been carrying in silence. The pressure to be strong, to be perfect, to be everything to everyone. You see the parts of me I hide behind my smile.

Show me where I am carrying things You never asked me to hold. Teach me how to lay some of this down without shame. Remind me that I am Your daughter before I am anyone's hero.

Give me courage to tell myself the truth and compassion to not judge myself for it. I thank You that my crown came from You, not from my suffering. Help me begin to Heal. In Jesus' name, Amen.

HER Move: This week, choose one thing you will not carry alone.

It does not have to be big to be holy. Here are some ideas:

- Ask for help with a task at work instead of silently doing it all.
- Delegate one household responsibility.

- Say no to an extra request you do not have the capacity for.
- Order food instead of cooking if you are truly exhausted.
- Tell someone you trust, "I am not okay, and I need support."

If you need words, try, I have a lot on my plate right now, and I need some help with this." Or "I am not able to take that on this week." Sis, I know- this might feel small to others, but for you, it is a crack in the wall. It is the beginning of shifting from "I carry it all" to "I get to be cared for too," you feel me. That is the first step of HER. Heal! Next, we will start unlearning survival mode that kept you alive once but is now keeping you from truly living.

CHAPTER 2

UNLEARNING SURVIVAL MODE

She didn't even realize she was holding her breath. Standing at the kitchen counter, scrolling through emails, answering a text, half-listening to somebody calling her name from the other room, thinking about tomorrow's meeting and next week's bills all at once... her chest was tight, jaw clenched, shoulders up near her ears.

Then she caught herself. Inhale. Exhale. Why did relaxing feel wrong? Sis, maybe this is you. The moment things get quiet; your brain starts making a list. If you sit down too long, you feel like you're "wasting time." If you're not fixing something for somebody, you feel useless. Rest feels suspicious. Peace feels unfamiliar. Calm feels like the setup before something goes wrong, girl!

That's not just a busy schedule. That's survival mode. What Survival Mode Looks Like: Survival mode isn't just about danger. It's what happens when your whole system is always bracing for the next hit. It can look like:

- **Hyper-productivity:** You can't sit still. You feel guilty doing "nothing." You only feel valuable when you're producing, achieving, or helping.
- **Constant alertness:** You're always scanning for what might go wrong at work, at home, in relationships. You rehearse arguments in your head. You replay conversations looking for what you said wrong.
- **Numbness:** You don't cry easily anymore. Not because nothing hurts, but because everything does, and you had to shut it down just to function.
- **People-pleasing:** You say yes fast and resent it later. You over-explain. You're terrified of disappointing people, so you over-give to stay "safe."
- **Self-neglect:** You'll move heaven and earth for everyone else, but your own needs keep getting pushed to "later." Doctor's appointments, rest, fun, dreams – always at the bottom.
  You know survival mode taught you to move like the world is always about to fall apart, and it's your job to keep it together, I feel you!

Where Survival Mode Came From? You didn't wake up one day and choose this. You learned it. For a lot of Black women, survival mode is generational. Maybe you saw a mama who worked two or three jobs and still made a way. A grandma who held the family together through loss, poverty, or migration. If it wasn't your mama or grandmother it may have been other female influences with the way most black families are structured, you may you had Aunties who never rested because "there's always work to do."

Maybe you had extended friends of the family where you grew up watching grown folks fall apart, so you became the stable one, took on adult responsibilities as a child: caring for siblings, solving problems, reading grown folks' emotions to stay out of trouble.

Hearing familiar instructions about how to prepare for navigating through life like, "You gotta be twice as good," "Don't give them a reason," "You can't mess up like them." Then add on experiences such as Racism that told you the world is not safe, Sexism that told you your "no" doesn't matter and Church or culture that praised you for being strong, long before you were ever allowed to be vulnerable.

Survival mode started as a gift. It helped you navigate unsafe spaces. It helped you get through seasons that would have crushed somebody else. Hear me when I say this, my point here is the key, what protected you then might be what's choking you now!

The Cost of Staying in Survival

Survival mode feels responsible. It feels like discipline. It feels like "being a good woman." But long-term, it has a price.

Emotionally:

- You struggle to feel joy without wondering when it will be snatched away.
- You downplay your wins because you're already focused on

the next threat.

- You confuse anxiety and urgency with "motivation."

Physically:

- Tension headaches, back and neck pain, poor sleep, digestive issues.
- Stress hormones on loop, body always in fight-flight-freeze.

Spiritually:

- You may even start to believe God is only pleased with you when you're hustling, grinding, serving, and suffering.
- Rest feels unholy. Receiving feels undeserved.

Relationally:

- You attract people who like how much you give; not how much you are.
- You feel resentful but don't know how to stop the pattern.
- You become the "strong friend" who never feels safe falling apart.

Professionally:

- You overwork without asking for what you're worth.
- You say yes to extra tasks instead of negotiating your role.
- People see your labor, but not your limits.

Sis, hear me when I say, survival got you here, but it cannot take you where you're going next. **God Didn't Call You Just To Survive!** Some of us were handed a theology of struggle.

We were given the idea—sometimes directly, sometimes between the lines—that suffering is holy, that exhaustion is proof of faithfulness, that if we're not pouring out to the point of emptiness, we're selfish. But open your Bible. Look at the life of Jesus, He slept in the middle of a storm, He withdrew from crowds even when needs were still present, He went away to pray, He didn't heal everybody everywhere and He said "no" to some demands because He was aligned with purpose, not pressured by people.

If Jesus, with all that power, allowed Himself to rest, to step away, to not fix every single thing in every single moment... why do you believe you're failing God if you do the same?

Survival mode says: "If I don't handle it, it will fall apart."

Faith says: "I'll do my part, but I am not God. The world is not held together by my exhaustion." that is the shift where healing starts.

Moving From Survival to Safety

Before you can thrive, you have to learn what safety even feels like. A lot of us think safety is just "no drama." But safety is deeper.

Emotional safety is:

- Being able to say how you feel without being punished or mocked.

- Knowing you won't be abandoned just for having a need.
- Not walking on eggshells in your own home or in your own head.

Physical safety is:

- Your body is not always bracing for impact.
- Having some stability: a place to rest, food to eat, basic needs met.
- Listening when your body says, "I'm done for today."

Spiritual safety is:

- Believing God is not waiting to punish you for resting.
- Trusting that you are loved even when you're not "useful."
- Feeling safe bringing your real feelings to God, not just the polished ones.

Practical safety can look like:

- A plan for your money instead of constant panic.
- Support systems: friends, therapist, community, mentors.
- Boundaries that protect your peace and time.

Survival mode told you, stay on edge. Stay ready and don't trust it when it's good. Healing invites you to ask, "What would it look like to actually feel safe in my own life?" Not safe because nothing bad ever happens. Safe because you're not facing life alone, empty, and pretending.

Honoring Survival, Releasing Its Control

I want you to hear this clearly, you don't have to hate who you were, to become who you're called to be. You can honor the version of you that showed up when nobody else did, protected the little girl inside you the only way she knew how and kept you alive emotionally, mentally, spiritually.

You can say, "Thank you, Survival Me. You did what you had to do. But we're safe enough now to try something different." Unlearning survival mode is not about shame. It's about permission, permission to try a slower pace without calling yourself lazy, ask for help without feeling weak, rest without earning it through suffering and enjoy good moments without waiting for the punishment. Sis, this is where HER(You) begin stretching her shoulders and realize that I'm not in the same war I was in 10 years ago, but I've still been moving like it. It's time to teach your nervous system, your mind, your spirit: "We are allowed to live, not just survive."

HER PRACTICE – *Chapter* 2
Unlearning Survival Mode

HER Reflection: Find a quiet moment and answer these as honestly as you can. No judgment. Just truth.

1. Where do you recognize survival mode in your life right now
   - Check what hits. Describe one situation where you see it the clearest:

- Overworking
- Always saying yes
- Never resting
- Always bracing for the worst
- Struggling to feel joy

2. When did you first learn you had to be "on guard". Write out that memory or time period. Be gentle with yourself as you remember
    - Was it something that happened in childhood
    - A moment you felt unsafe, unseen, or unprotected
    - A season where you had to grow up fast

3. What do you believe would happen if you stopped living in survival mode, finish these sentences:
    - "If I slow down, I'm afraid that..."
    - "If I ask for help, I'm afraid that..."
    - "If I rest, I'm afraid that..."

4. Where does your life show signs of safety that your mind hasn't caught up to yet? Name 3 ways your life is safer now than it used to be, even if it's not perfect. Sis, I need you to be real honest on that page when you reflect back. That honesty is holy!
    - Are you more stable now than you were 5 years ago
    - Do you have more resources, wisdom, or support now

HER Prayer

"God, I thank You for getting me through seasons I didn't think I'd survive. Thank You for the strength I had when I felt alone, for the times You carried me even when I didn't know it was You.

God, I also confess that I don't always know how to live outside of survival. Being on edge has felt normal. Waiting for the worst has felt like protection. Today, I bring You my fear of slowing down, my fear of resting, my fear of not being the strong one all the time. Show me where I am safe now. Show me where I can lay my weapons down. Teach my body, my mind, and my spirit how to trust You in calm seasons, not just in crisis. Help me honor the parts of me that learned to survive, while giving Your Spirit permission to teach me how to really live. I release the belief that I am only valuable when I am struggling, hustling, or fixing. I am Your daughter, even when I am still. Even when I am receiving. Even when I am resting. Heal my nervous system. Heal my patterns. Heal my pace. In Jesus' name, Amen."

HER Move: This week, I want you to do one small thing that gently tells your body "We are learning a new way." Pick ONE of these, or create your own:

- Micro-rest ritual: Set a timer for 5–10 minutes. Sit or lie down. No phone. No multitasking. Breathe slowly. When guilt thoughts pop up, tell yourself, "I am allowed to rest."

Say no once, on purpose: When someone asks you to do something you truly don't have the capacity for, practice saying, "I don't have the space to take that on right now." Then don't over-explain.

- Change one survival habit into a safety habit:
- Survival: skipping meals because you're "too busy."
- Safety: sit and eat one meal without working at the same time.
- Survival: answering every text right away like it's an emergency.
- Safety: respond when you are available, not on demand.
- - Bedtime boundary: Choose a time to stop working, scrolling, or planning. Call it your "HER Cutoff." After that time, you don't solve the world. You let God be God. Sis, it might feel awkward at first. That's okay. You're not failing. You're re-training.

Every time you choose safety over survival, you are whispering to that younger version of you, "We're not in danger anymore. We're allowed to live differently now." This is what healing looks like in motion. Heal. Unlearn survival. Make room for HER to breathe.

CHAPTER 3

HEALING THE STORY IN HER HEAD

There are the facts of your life, and- then there's the story you tell yourself about those facts, they may sound something like this:

- **Fact:** He didn't text back.
- **Story:** "I'm not worth choosing."
- **Fact:** You didn't get the promotion.
- **Story:** "I'm not as good as I thought. I should just be grateful I even have a job."
- **Fact:** Your parent/s criticized you growing up.
- **Story:** "I am always messing up. I have to be perfect to be loved."

Most of the pain we carry day to day doesn't come from what happened—it comes from what we decided it meant about us. We're going deeper, stay with me! This chapter is about that quiet narrator in your mind, the one who's been talking over God for years.

The Voice In Her Head

She was replaying the conversation for the twentieth time. It wasn't a big thing on the outside. Just a comment from her boss in a meeting: "We're not sure you're quite ready for that level yet." Everybody kept talking like nothing happened. But in her head, a whole storm started. The voices replay over and over, "See You're not really leadership material, "You sounded dumb," "You should have kept quiet," or "You're not like them. You're just here to do the work, not to lead." By the time she got home, it wasn't even about the comment anymore. It was about every time she'd ever felt dismissed, unseen, or "too much." The story in her head had turned one sentence into a whole identity. Maybe you know that feeling where one "no" echoes like "never," one failure feels like "forever," one rejection becomes "I am the problem." Sis, you know- that's not God talking. That's the old story.

The Stories She Learned To Believe

Let's name some of the common stories Black women carry in our minds:

- "I have to work twice as hard just to be seen as average."
- "If I mess up once, they will never forget."
- "I am too loud, too opinionated, too emotional."
- "I'm not as smart as them, I just work harder."
- "I'm not leadership material, I'm support."
- "If I don't hold it together, everything falls apart."

- "Nobody really shows up for me the way I show up for them."
- "I should be further along by now."

These beliefs sit so deep, we stop seeing them as stories and start treating them like truth. But ask yourself, who told you that, when did you first hear that message, and who benefits from you believing that about yourself? You weren't born thinking you were "too much" or "not enough." Somebody, somewhere, taught you that!

Where Those Stories Came From

A lot of our inner story comes from the people, places, and things that we place value. Let's begin with **Family**, our parents or caregivers who were hard on you where being praised only when you performed or achieved or being compared to siblings or cousins.

School, perhaps you experiences were with teachers who underestimated you or overdisciplined you. You may have suffered being called "talkative," "disruptive," or "bossy" when you were just expressive or smart.

Church, where the key messages were those that centered sacrifice but not self-worth and being taught to serve but not to have needs.

Culture & Media today has done a disservice to Black Women. When will it stop? Seeing Black women portrayed as loud, angry, oversexualized, or invisible we are not seeing women who look like you in positions of softness and power.

Workplaces are oftentimes the loudest, being the only Black woman in the room or being complimented for "how well you handle things" but never fully invested in.

Over time, all of that becomes a script. You walk into rooms not as a blank slate, but as someone carrying a whole narrative: "They probably already think I'm less than. I better prove I deserve to be here." Sis, that script might have helped you navigate spaces, but now it's running your whole inner world.

The Problem With An Unhealed Story

An unhealed story doesn't just hurt your feelings—it shapes your choices. If your story is, "I'm lucky to even be here," then you, don't negotiate, don't ask for clarity, don't set boundaries and you accept the bare minimum. If your story is, "Nobody really stays," then you don't fully open up, sabotage closeness and you choose emotionally unavailable people so you're never "surprised." If your story is, "I'm too much," then you, shrink your ideas, edit your personality, quiet your voice in meetings, at church, in friendships. Lastly, If your story is, "I'm not enough," then you, overcompensate, overwork, and over give. The story in your head becomes the ceiling on your life. What God Says vs. What The Story Says let's be clear, the story in your head is not automatically truth, your feelings are real, but the meaning you attach to them might be off.

Stay with me here: **Your story might say;** "You're always behind." **God says:** You are fearfully and wonderfully made." "I know the plans I have for you." "I make everything beautiful in its time."

Your story might say: "You're too broken to be used." **God says:** "My strength is made perfect in weakness." "Nothing can separate you from My love." "I'll use all things for your good."

Your story might say: "You have to prove you're worthy." **God says:** "You were chosen before the foundation of the world." "You are My workmanship." "You are loved with an everlasting love."

Sis, both voices can't be Lord of your life at the same time. At some point, you have to decide whose story am I going to live by. ***Healing Doesn't Erase The Past, It Rewrites The Meaning.*** Healing the story in your head doesn't mean pretending the harm never happened. It means changing what it means about you now. Example:

Old story: "My father left, so I must not be worth staying for." **Healed story:** "My father left, and that hurt deeply. But his choice was about his wounds, not my worth. God has never left me, and I am still worthy of love that stays."

Old story: "They didn't promote me because I'm not good enough." **Healed story:** "They didn't promote me. That's data about them and that environment, not the final verdict on my destiny. I will keep growing, advocating for myself, and if I outgrow this place, I will go where I am valued."

Old story: "I was abused, so I must be dirty, broken, or unlovable." **Healed story:** "I was harmed, and it was not my fault. The shame belongs to the person who did it, not me. God still sees me as pure, loved, and redeemable."

Do you see the difference? The facts remain, but the meaning shifts. That shift is where chains start to fall. When you begin writing a New Story with God, you are not stuck with the narrative you inherited. You can confront the lies.

CHAPTER 4

WOMEN BEFORE HER, GOD, AND THE WOMAN IN THE MIRROR

She was standing in the bathroom, edge control in one hand, scarf in the other, trying to get her hair to do what she wanted, not what it wanted. She caught her reflection and paused. For a second, she didn't see "today her" at all. She saw flashes of faces, Her grandmother at the stove. Her mother getting ready for work before the sun came up. Her aunt at the kitchen table, paying bills with a stack of envelopes and a tired smile.

Same eyes. Same nose. Same cheekbones. Same determined set of the mouth when life was life-ing. She looked at herself and thought, "Am I really living... or am I just continuing what they had to survive" Sis, maybe you've had that mirror moment, I am speaking of. You look at your face and see everybody else's sacrifices. You feel grateful—and also a little bit guilty for wanting more. This chapter is about holding all three truths at once, the Women who carried you, the God who created you, and the woman in the mirror who still has a life to live.

The Shoulders She Stands On

Before you ever knew your own name, someone was calling your future out in prayer. A grandmother whispering, "Lord, cover my babies." A mama saying, "My child is gonna be somebody." An ancestor on a plantation, or a field, or a small town, or a city bus, thinking, "Maybe my granddaughter won't have to go through this." Sis, you are not random. You are continuation.

Think about it, somebody worked jobs that broke their back so you could have choices. Somebody kept food on the table when they had no idea how it would stretch. Somebody swallowed their own dreams so you could chase yours. My goodness, that's a lot of history sitting in your DNA. You stand on! In your bloodline there were women who weren't allowed to vote. Women who were told "education isn't for you." Women who were brilliant but never got titles. We definitely don't want to leave out the women who were spiritual leaders in their homes and communities, even if nobody gave them a microphone. Trust me when I say this, you are living in answers they never got to see.

Gratitude Without Guilt

Here's where it gets tricky. Sometimes, when Black women talk about "the women before them" and "sacrifice," it quietly turns into pressure. We are dismissive of our today struggles to be, by replaying the thoughts of "They went through worse, so I shouldn't complain." "I have opportunities they didn't have, so I better not mess up." "They survived all that, and I'm over here tired from emails I can send from my phone." You end up minimizing your own pain because it doesn't look like theirs. Do you realize that two truths can sit side by side? Listen, sis, your grandmother might have survived segregation, and you are still allowed to be hurt by being the only Black woman in the boardroom. Your mother might have worked two jobs, and you are still allowed to feel exhausted by holding everything together by yourself, the impact of emotional labor and microaggressions for some are a real, reality.

Your ancestors might have fought to simply stay alive, and you are still allowed to want more than survival. Honoring them does not mean replicating their suffering. Sis, trust and believe me when I say gratitude does not require you to stay in bondage, they would have walked out of those tough places if they could.

God, the women before, And You

Let's be real clear, you are here because God created you, on purpose. You are also here because your people survived enough storms to keep your bloodline going.

Those are not enemies. That's alignment. God used imperfect people, in hard conditions, to carry you to this moment. But God is not just the God of your past. He is the God of your becoming. Your ancestors were not your savior. They were your lineage.

God is the One who formed you, called you, and put purpose in you for this generation. The women before you / ancestors remind you that you're not alone, they show you survival and strength through the life they lived. God on the other hand, defines your identity, directs your purpose, and heals what history harmed. And then there's you, the place where past, present, and future all meet in one body.

The Woman In The Mirror

Now, we come back to that reflection. When you look in the mirror, what do you see first Flaws or features, Past or potential, Everybody else... or you? A lot of Black women have a complicated relationship with the mirror; they are the years of being told your skin was "too dark" or "too light." Comments about your nose, lips, hair, body. But then there is Beauty standards that did not include faces like yours. Also add, Spiritual pressure to "Be humble, don't be vain." Coupled with social pressure to "Be flawless at all times." My goodness, no wonder some of us only look closely at ourselves to fix something, whether it be to Clean up, Cover up, or Correct focusing on the perfected images we are constantly trying to live up to. But what if the mirror could become a sacred place instead of a battlefield? What if you looked in it and saw a woman God handcrafted. A living answer to prayers. Someone worthy of care, not just correction. Sis, healing includes healing how you see yourself in that glass, you feel me.

Becoming HER In Front Of The Glass

Remember our framework: Healing · Evolving · Rising. This is where your thought process changes. It's time to come face to face with the influences of your past and present. In front of the mirror, this is what that looks like:

Healing: Acknowledge the hurtful messages you've absorbed about your appearance, your Blackness, your womanhood. Let yourself grieve the times you tried to shrink or erase yourself.

Evolving: Begin speaking to yourself with kindness, the way you would to a daughter or little sister. Start shifting from "What's wrong with me" to "What is beautiful, powerful, and unique about me"

Rising: Own your presence. Walk out the house like, "I am not an accident. I am an assignment." Show up in rooms as the fullness of who you are, not just the edited version.

When you stand in front of that mirror, you are standing, with your ancestors at your back, with God's hand on your life, and with your own eyes choosing how to see yourself. That's holy ground!

HER PRACTICE - *Chapter 4*

The Women Before, God, And The Woman In The Mirror

HER Reflection: Take a moment when you're alone, preferably somewhere you can see yourself—a mirror, front camera, or even just a quiet corner to visualize.

1. Your lineage: Write down the names (or roles) of 3 women whose shoulders you stand on. They can be:
    - women in your family (mother, grandmother, aunt, godmother)
    - women from history
    - or unnamed ancestors you just feel in your spirit
    - Next to each name, write one sentence:
    - "Because of her, I..."

   Example:
    - "Because of my grandmother, I know resilience."
    - "Because of my mother, I know how to work."
    - "Because of my aunt, I know how to pray."

2. The weight and the gift. For each of those women, ask:
    - "What beautiful thing did I inherit from her"
    - "What heavy thing might I be carrying that she had to carry, but I don't have to anymore"

3. Your mirror story. When you look in the mirror, what are the first 3 thoughts that usually come to your mind , be honest and write them down:

- Are they kind or critical
- Are they about appearance only, or about your whole self

4. God's view. If God were standing behind you, looking at you in the mirror, what do you believe He would say about you? Write a few phrases that feel true to His character, take your time, don't rush this. Let it breathe:
    - "That's my daughter."
    - "She is loved."
    - "I'm proud of how far she's come."
    - "I'm not finished with her yet."

HER *Prayer*

You can pray this while looking at yourself in the mirror, or with eyes closed if that's more comfortable. "God, I thank You for the women who came before me—named and unnamed—who endured, survived, and sacrificed so I could stand here today. I honor the mothers, grandmothers, aunties, and ancestors in my bloodline and in my community. I thank You for their strength, their faith, their creativity and their fight.

At the same time, I confess that sometimes I feel crushed by the weight of what they carried. I've believed that I have to struggle the way they did in order to be worthy. I've minimized my own pain because I told myself, 'They had it worse.'

Today, I release the guilt that keeps me from wanting more. I believe, You are big enough to honor their sacrifice and give me rest, joy, and abundance. As I look at myself, heal my vision. Heal the way I see my face, my body, my Blackness, my womanhood. Let me see what You see when You look at me. Show me how to live in a way that honors the women before me, not by repeating their suffering, but by receiving the freedom they prayed for. Teach me to stand in the mirror and say, 'I am loved. I am chosen. I am HER.' In Jesus' name, Amen."

HER Move: This week, we're going to make the mirror a little less hostile and a little more holy.

1. Mirror moment ritual (3–5 minutes). Once a day, stand in front of a mirror (or use your phone camera if that's all you've got).
    - Look yourself in the eyes. Really look.
    - Breathe slowly, in and out, a few times.
    - Then say out loud (even if it feels awkward):
    - "I come from women who survived a lot. I honor them."
    - "But I am not only their survival. I am God's daughter."
    - "I am more than what I do for others."
    - "I am worthy of love, rest, and joy."
    - "I am HER: healing, evolving, rising."

2. Ancestral gratitude without bondage.
    - Write a short note or prayer that starts with:
    - "To the women who came before me..."
    - Thank them for specific things.

Then add:

- "I promise to..."

and complete it with a commitment that reflects freedom, not more chains.

Example:

- "I promise to live fully, not just survive."
- "I promise to rest when I'm tired."
- "I promise to use my voice where you didn't have one."

3. One visual reminder. Place one item somewhere you'll see it—a photo of an ancestor, a piece of jewelry, a word on a sticky note like "HER" or "Daughter." Let it remind you:
    - You're supported by more than what you can see.
    - You're loved by God more than you can measure.

Sis, every time you walk past that mirror or that reminder and choose to see yourself with a little more love, you're healing a story that's older than you—and writing a better one for the women coming after you, this is HER work. Heal the line. Honor the past. See the woman in the mirror as worthy of a different future. I am excited to be on this journey with you.

CHAPTER 5

BOUNDARIES AS A SPIRITUAL ACT

By the time she finally sat down on the edge of the bed, her phone was still lighting up. "Can you talk real quick," "Hey, can you help me with...," "Did you see my email," "Are you still coming"... Her body said no hours ago. Her spirit said no yesterday. Her mouth kept saying, "Yeah, I got you." She stared at the screen and thought, "If I say no, they're gonna be disappointed. They're gonna think I'm selfish. They're gonna stop asking me. They're gonna..."Then she caught it. When did "no" become a sin? When did "tired" stop being a good enough reason? When did everybody else's peace become more important than hers? Sis, if that hits your chest a little, this chapter is for you, Lets, dig in!

Why Boundaries Feel So Wrong (Especially For Us)

A lot of Black women were not raised to have boundaries. We were raised to, help, fix, serve, be grateful, make it work, and "Do what you gotta do." At one or a few times in our lives you might have also heard, girl, "Don't be rude, " "Don't talk back," "You better help when grown folks ask." Or "You got an attitude now" just for having a different opinion. Whew! Then to add church and culture, you gotta "be a servant," "put others before yourself." All this under the heart-stained banner of being good woman sacrifices.

Nobody told you the difference between sacrifice led by the Spirit and self-neglect shaped by guilt. So now when you're exhausted, you still say yes. How about when your calendar is full, you still squeeze people in? What about the times when your heart is hurting, you still pour into everybody else? And when you even think about saying no, You feel guilty, You feel mean, or you feel like a bad daughter / wife / friend / church member.

Let's pause here for a moment, think about it, that's not conviction from God, that's conditioning, it's important to know the difference.

What Boundaries Actually Are (And Are Not)

Let's clear this up. Boundaries are-limits you set around your time, energy, body, emotions, and resources. They are ways of saying, "This is what I can do. This is what I cannot do." They are also acts of self-respect and clarity, not punishment. What boundaries are not- walls that mean you don't love people, revenge, payback, or silent treatment last they are not "Un-Christian" or "unloving."

Think of a boundary like the fence around a house: you still let people in, but there is a gate. The banks of a river: they don't stop the water, they direct it, so it doesn't flood everything. without boundaries, you become resentful (doing things you don't really want to do), You become burnt out (giving from an empty well). Listen, its true that you cannot pour from an empty cup. Giving yourself, permission to not overextend is necessary to reduce the misunderstanding of when enough is enough. To clarify, you become confused (unsure where you end and other people begin).

With boundaries you can love people honestly, not from a place of quiet bitterness. You can serve from overflow, not depletion. You can show up as your full self, not a doormat version. Jesus created boundaries and showed us acts of kindness by being "Nice" however that wasn't always the case. For whatever reason we act like Jesus was a 24/7 yes man. He wasn't! - He withdrew from crowds when He was tired. - He went away to pray even when people still had needs. - He didn't heal everybody in every town. - He said things that disappointed people who wanted Him to fit their expectations.

It is true that Jesus loved deeply. He gave generously. BUT He also stayed aligned with purpose, not people-pleasing. If Jesus can have boundaries and still be Love in the flesh, you can have boundaries and still be a loving Black woman, God is not honored by, you being used, drained, manipulated, or abused in His name.

Boundaries are not you turning away from God; they are you turning away from idolatry of other people's approval. Sometimes "no" is the most spiritual word you can say.

Where You Need Boundaries

Let's get specific. Where are your lines blurry maybe for you it at work, you often find yourself being the unofficial therapist for your coworkers, taking on extra tasks without pay or clear credit, answering emails/texts/calls at all hours or letting microaggressions slide until you're full of quiet rage.

Possible boundaries can be in your availability and time management. Its ok to say, "I'm not available after __pm for work calls," or "I can support with this, but I won't be taking on additional unpaid responsibilities." And how about, "I don't appreciate comments like that. Let's keep it professional."

At home and with family- Being the default babysitter, driver, lender, planner, fixer, being pulled into every argument, or carrying everybody's secrets and problems. It's ok the say to your loved ones: "I can't talk about that right now. It's draining for me," "I love you, but I'm not able to take that on this time," or "I'm not comfortable being in the middle of this conflict."

In relationships (romantic and friendships)- Overgiving to people who under-give. You are always being the one to call, text, plan, apologize and tolerating disrespect because you're scared to be alone. People need to hear you say: "I need mutual effort in this relationship. Right now, it feels one-sided," and "speaking to me like that is not okay. If it continues, I'll have to step back," and "If we can't communicate respectfully, I'm going to end this conversation here." If they love you they will respect you and your boundaries.

The boundaries With Yourself are the most difficult but the most important. Look! saying "tomorrow" to your own rest, health, and dreams every single day and letting everybody else's emergencies outrun your priorities, is a health crisis in the making. Sis, boundaries are not just about saying no to others, they're about saying yes to you, and its ok! Yes, "after this time, I stop working and start resting." No, "I will not cancel my therapy/doctor/rest time for non-emergencies," and from here on out, "I get to say yes to me, even if no one else is asking." Trust me folks are going to figure things out for themselves!

Preparing For The Pushback

Here's the thing nobody tells you: When you start setting boundaries, the people who benefited from you having none... will not clap. Some will say you've changed (you have, that's the point). Some will try to guilt you: "Oh, you too good now." Some will test the boundary to see if you really mean it.

That doesn't mean the boundary is wrong. It means the dynamic is being exposed. You are not responsible for their disappointment, their tantrums, or their refusal to understand. You are responsible for, stewarding your health, honoring your limits, and listening to God about your capacity. Here is the truth of the matter, every "no" that protects your purpose is also a "yes" to what God actually assigned to you, you feel me.

HER PRACTICE – *Chapter* 5
Boundaries As A Spiritual Act

HER Reflection: Get your journal and answer these with full honesty. No editing to sound nice. Resentment is often a sign that a boundary is needed or has been crossed.

1. Where do you feel the most resentment right now
    - Work, family, church, friendships, relationship
2. What did you learn about saying "no" growing up
    - Were you allowed to disagree with adults
    - Were you shamed when you tried to speak up
    - Did you see any woman in your life have healthy boundaries
3. What are you afraid will happen if you start setting real boundaries, complete these:
    - "If I start saying no more often, I'm scared that..."
    - "If I stop being always available, people will..."
    - "If I ask for what I need, they might..."
4. What have boundaries cost you so far (or the lack of them) This is the part where you need to be raw. That truth is your starting point:

- Has it cost you peace
- Has it harmed your body (stress, illness, burnout)
- Has it affected your relationship with God because you're serving from emptiness?

HER *Prayer*

"God, You see how often I have confused love with overextending myself. You know the times I have said yes on the outside while crying no on the inside. You know the messages I was taught—that a good woman, a good daughter, a good wife, a good friend, a good Christian always says yes, always shows up, always gives, no matter how she feels. Today, I bring You my fear of disappointing people. I bring You my guilt around rest. I bring You the part of me that believes my value is in what I do for everybody else.

Jesus, You had boundaries. You took time away. You went off to pray. You didn't meet every demand. Help me believe that I can follow Your example without being selfish. Show me where I need to set new boundaries. Give me the words to say them clearly and kindly. Give me the courage to hold them, even when people push back.

Teach me that saying no, when You are not leading me to yes, is obedience, not rebellion. I trust that You will still take care of the people I can't carry. I trust that You will still love me when I put the weight down. I trust that I am more than my usefulness. In Jesus' name, Amen."

HER Move: Now we move from theory to action, gently but clearly. This week, you're going to:

1. Choose ONE boundary to set or strengthen. Pick one area:
    - Work
    - Family
    - Church/community
    - Friendship
    - Romantic relationship

   Ask: "What is one small but real boundary I can set this week that would honor my energy and my purpose" Examples:
    - "I will not answer work emails after 7pm."
    - "I will not loan money that I cannot afford to give."
    - "I will not say yes on the spot; I will say, 'Let me get back to you.'"
    - "I will not listen to hours of venting when I am emotionally drained."

2. Use a simple script. When the moment comes, try one of these:
    - The pause script: "Let me check my schedule and get back to you."
    - (Buys you time so you don't yes out of pressure.)
    - The gentle no: "I'm not able to take that on right now."
    - The redirect: "I care about you, but I'm not in the space to talk about this deeply tonight."
    - The boundary with reason (if needed): "I need to start

logging off work by 6pm for my own health, so I won't be replying to messages after that. "You do not owe a whole essay. Clarity is kindness.

3. Journal what happens—inside and outside. After you hold that boundary:
    - How did your body feel
    - Did you feel guilty, relieved, scared, powerful
    - How did the other person respond

Write it down. Then remind yourself:

- "I am allowed to protect my time, energy, and peace."
- "The people who truly love me will adjust."
- "The ones who only loved my lack of boundaries are not my measuring stick."

Sis, this is not about becoming hard or cold. It's about becoming honest; you owe it to yourself. Every healthy boundary you set is another step out of burnout and another step toward the HER you're becoming: A woman who can love deeply without losing herself in the process.

Part II

EVOLVING

Becoming the Woman She Envisions In Her Spirit

CHAPTER 6

FROM PEOPLE-PLEASING TO PURPOSE-LED

She heard herself say it before she could stop it "Yeah, that's fine. I can do it." Her stomach dropped right after the words left her mouth. She had just agreed to stay late at work... again, take on a project that wasn't really her job, or miss the quiet evening she'd promised herself.

Why did that "yes" come out faster than her truth? Why did protecting their comfort feel more urgent than protecting her own peace? On the way home, the real conversation started—inside her head, "I didn't want to do that." "I'm tired." "I should've said no." "Now I'm mad... but at who Them Or me?"

Sis, hear me when I say this- if you've ever been angry at yourself for the yes you didn't mean, you're in the right chapter, just stay with me, we are going somewhere! This is where we start shifting from people-pleasing to purpose-led living. What People-Pleasing Really Is (And What It's Not). People-pleasing is not just "being nice." It's when you say yes when your spirit is screaming no, change yourself to avoid someone else's discomfort, agree just to keep the peace, even when you feel disturbed inside.

It can look like laughing at a joke that wasn't funny—or wasn't okay, taking on extra work to "prove" you're a team player, always being available, even when you're exhausted, never stating what you want—"I'm good with whatever." At its root, people-pleasing is fear in a cute outfit, fear of rejection, - conflict, not being liked, being called "difficult," or not being chosen or included. It's survival mode with makeup on!

Where People-Pleasing Came From

You didn't wake up one day and decide, "I want to betray myself for a living." You learned that being pleasing = being safe. Maybe, at home, love felt conditional when you got attention when you were helpful, quiet, obedient, and high-achieving. However, when you expressed a boundary, you were told you had "an attitude." At school, teachers praised you for being "so mature," "so well-behaved," "so responsible." You saw what happened to the "loud" kids, the "rebellious" ones... and you learned to float under the radar.

In relationships, you got abandoned or punished when you stood up for yourself. You learned to bend so you wouldn't be left. As a Black woman in the world, you clocked how quickly people label you "angry," "intimidating," "ungrateful," "too much" you internalized a rule, if I keep them comfortable, maybe I'll be safe. So, you crafted a version of yourself that fit, agreeable, accommodating, low-maintenance, endlessly understanding. Sis, I know, trust me, the cost has been high! It's what I refer to as "The Hidden Cost Of Keeping Everyone Happy." Let's look at the truth of what people-pleasing does;

Emotionally:

- You feel resentful but can't always explain why.
- You feel unseen because no one knows what you really think or need.
- You feel tired from carrying everyone's comfort.

Spiritually:

- You start confusing "being Christ-like" with having no boundaries, no opinions, no edges, ultimately no voice.
- You apologize to God more for saying no to people than you do for saying no to Him.

Relationally:

- You attract takers, fixers, and users.
- You feel guilty when you're not fixing somebody.
- You stay longer in relationships (romantic, friendships, jobs) than your peace can afford.

Identity-wise:

- You don't fully know what you want anymore.
- You lose touch with your own desires, preferences, dreams.

Purpose-wise:

- You are so busy reacting to other people's needs that you haven't had time to ask, "God, what did You actually put me here to do?"

Sis, I know, people-pleasing feels holy, but it keeps you from your promised land. Please know the difference in *Pleasing People* vs. *Loving People*. Why is this important? We are called to love people, not to worship their approval. Loving people is honest, has boundaries, and sometimes disappoints them for their good or yours. People-pleasing lies to keep the peace, over-extends, and sacrifices your calling on the altar of "no hard feelings." Love may say, "I care about you, but I can't do that for you." People-pleasing says ,"I'll do it, even if it hurts me, so you don't think I'm a bad person." Love asks "God, what are You asking me to do here?" People-pleasing asks, "What will they think of me if I don't?"

Can you see the differences between the two, one is led by purpose, and the other is led by fear. Let me explain, Purpose-Led, you are probable wondering what does that even mean. To be purpose-led means, you know your life has assignment, not just activity. You make choices by asking, "Does this align with who God says I am and what He's calling me to do?" You serve, give, love—but from a place of clarity, not compulsion.

Purpose-led living sounds like, "I love y'all, but I can't be everything to everyone, "I need to pray on that before committing," "that's not aligned with where God is taking me" and "I'm called to more than just keeping everybody comfortable." In other words, it doesn't mean you never help, never show up, never do things that stretch you it means, simply this, you are no longer driven by the fear of being disliked, you are driven by the desire to be faithful. **HER** is not rude... but she is not ruled by God.

Practical Shifts: From "Yes Girl" To Aligned Woman

This isn't about flipping a switch overnight. It's about small, steady shifts, which will look like this when put into practice: One, from automatic yes to intentional pauses, the people-pleasing reflex will say "yes" the second someone asks, but the purpose-led move is going to insert a pause and respond in a New habit phrases such as these:

- "Let me check my schedule and get back to you."
- "I need to think and pray on that."
- "I'll let you know by tomorrow."

That tiny pausc gives your spirit time to speak before your fear does. You will go from "What will they think" to "What is God saying." In the beginning that old filter will rise up and replay the conversation "If I say no, will they be mad/disappointed" but your new filter will remind you that "If I say yes, am I disobeying what God's been telling me about rest, focus, or my calling", this action is your surrender to shifting the throne from them back to Him.

Now let's consider going from avoiding conflict to allowing honest conversations, the old story will replay "If I disagree, they'll leave or think I'm difficult," but your new story, will respond "If this connection can't handle honesty, it's not as solid as I thought." I know that you don't go looking for fights, but you have to stop bending yourself into silence to avoid them.

When we have adult children it's so hard to go from everybody's fixer to steward of your lane. We as women have seen this role lived out to the point of exhaustion and oftentimes the old mode is so ingrained, that we wear *Super SHEROE Everybody Fixer* title as a badge of honor. That old mode has you stuck in "If there's a problem, it must be my job to solve it." I am telling you, renew your mind in this area, adapt the new mode by asking yourself, "Is this mine to carry Or am I stepping into God's spot?"

Purpose-led women ask, "Is this my assignment, or am I just addicted to being needed?" You know, real talk, needing to be needed is a quiet addiction. Understand me when I say, you're allowed to disappoint people! This might be one of the hardest truths. Trust and believe, you will inevitably disappoint someone when you start living honestly.

It may begin with the friend who liked you better when you never said no, the coworker who loved you being the team mule. The family member who expects you to drop everything, every time. But ask yourself, Is it better for them to be temporarily disappointed, or you to live permanently disobedient to your purpose? Some disappointments are actually divine separation. Some people are in love with your performance, not your person.

Purpose-led living might cost you some fake peace, some fake relationships, some fake versions of you. But it will return to you your self-respect, your inner alignment, your capacity for the calling on your life. Sis, let me tell you, HER is not for everybody's comfort, she's for God's assignment.

HER PRACTICE - *Chapter 6*
From People-Pleasing To Purpose-Led

HER Reflection: Take your time with these. This is identity work.

1. Where do you people-please the most and describe one recent moment where you said yes but wanted to say no. Circle or write:
    - Work
    - Family
    - Romantic relationships
    - Friendships
    - Church/community
2. What are you usually afraid of when you say no or set a limit? Notice what comes up: rejection, anger, abandonment, gossip, etc. Complete:
    - "If I say no, I'm scared they will…"
    - "If I'm honest about what I need, I'm scared they'll…"

Notice what comes up: rejection, anger, abandonment, gossip, etc.

3. What did you learn about being "a good woman" or "a good Christian" Write about the messages you absorbed:
    - Were you taught that good women never complain, always help, always say yes
    - Did you see any women in your life model healthy no's
4. What might your life look like if you were truly purpose-led instead of people-pleasing? Close your eyes and imagine, Jot down whatever you see, this is you telling yourself the truth.:
    - How would you spend your time
    - Who would you stop chasing
    - What would you finally start

HER *Prayer*

"God, you see how often I have traded your 'well done' for their 'thank you.' You know the times I said yes with my mouth while my heart was saying no. The times I betrayed myself just to keep someone else comfortable. The times I confused being loving with being a doormat. Today, I confess that I have allowed the fear of people's opinions to lead me more than I've allowed your purpose to lead me. I bring you my fear of rejection, my fear of being called difficult, my fear of being left out or left behind. Dear God, remind me that I am already accepted in you. I am already loved, not for my performance but for who I am as your daughter. Teach me to pause before I answer. Teach me to ask, 'Lord, is this mine to do.' Teach me to obey your yes and your no.

Give me courage to disappoint people when necessary, without hating them and without hating myself. Let my life be led by purpose, not pressured by people. Help me become the woman you had in mind when you made me—not the version everyone else is most comfortable with, but the version that is most aligned with You. In Jesus' name, Amen."

HER Move: Now we practice one small shift from people-pleasing to purpose-led.

1. Choose ONE relationship or space to practice in this week. Write their name or the setting down. Pick the area where your yes comes fastest:
    - Maybe it's that coworker who always dumps stuff on you.
    - Maybe it's that friend who vents for hours.
    - Maybe it's a family member who expects instant access.

2. Decide your new boundary or pause. Keep it simple and specific.

   Examples:

- "I will not give an answer on the spot. I'll say, 'Let me think and get back to you.'"
- "I will not stay later than my agreed hours this week."
- "I will not take emotionally heavy calls after 9pm."
- "I will not agree to events on my only rest day without

praying on it first."

3. Use your purpose-led phrase. When the moment comes, try something like:
    - "I appreciate you thinking of me, but I'm not able to do that this time."
    - "I want to show up well, so I need to check my capacity and get back to you."
    - "I'm focusing on some things God has me working on, so I can't take on anything extra right now." Then—this is key—do not backtrack the first time they sigh, act disappointed, or say, "But it's just..." You're building a new muscle.

4. Journal the aftermath. Afterward, ask yourself:
    - How did I feel after honoring my boundary
    - (Scared Relieved Powerful Guilty All of the above)
    - Did anything actually fall apart
    - What did I learn about myself
    - What might God be showing me through this

Take a moment write it out. Let it be data, not drama. Every time you choose purpose over people-pleasing, you're telling your soul, "We don't live for their approval anymore. We live from God's love and into God's assignment." Sis, this is where EVOLVING really starts—you begin walking like the healed woman you met in Part I, HEALING taught you to tell the truth about your pain. EVOLVING is going to teach you to live from your power.

CHAPTER 7

FROM "GRATEFUL TO BE HERE" TO "I BELONG HERE

She sat in the meeting, notebook open, pen in hand, heart beating just a little too fast. She had ideas. Real ones. She'd been up the night before thinking through solutions, connecting dots nobody else seemed to see. But when it was time to speak, something in her chest whispered, "Just be grateful you're even in the room. Don't mess it up. "So, she stayed quiet. Later, someone else tossed out a lighter version of the very idea she'd been sitting on. Everybody nodded. "Great point." "Love that." "Let's try that." She smiled on the outside. But, on the inside: "That could've been me" she thought to herself. Have you ever been there, Sis?

The room you prayed to be in... now has you shrinking in the corner, you feel me. This chapter is about that shift from "I'm lucky they let me be here" to "I was meant to be here."

The "Grateful To Be Here" Trap

Gratitude is beautiful. But gratitude, twisted by insecurity, becomes a trap. It sounds like, "I'm just happy they gave me a chance." "I don't want to rock the boat." "I don't want to seem ungrateful by asking for more." "I'm just blessed to have a seat, that's enough." And underneath that, "I'm not sure I actually deserve this." Unfortunately, as black women, we're often taught to be thankful for crumbs because someone somewhere had none. So, when we get a job our grandmother couldn't have, sit at tables our mother wasn't invited to, make money or moves our family never saw before, we can feel guilty wanting anything beyond bare minimum access. We confuse "I'm grateful" with "I'll accept whatever you give and never ask for what's fair."

How Black Women Learn To Shrink In Big Rooms

Let's name some layers. From early on, a lot of us were taught, "Don't be too loud." "Don't embarrass us." "You gotta work twice as hard to get half as far." "Don't give them a reason." What does that translate to, stay polished, stay perfect, Stay small. Then you step into, school & workspaces where you might be the only Black woman where your intelligence is questioned until "proven." Where your confidence is called "attitude," but for the other people it's called "leadership." After enough, being interrupted, being overlooked, - being praised privately but never publicly, you start to breathe smaller in rooms, apologizing before you speak, putting "just" in your emails ("Just checking in, just wanted to say…"), waiting to see how everyone else reacts before you offer your thought. Have you ever felt as if your body is in the room, but your spirit is in the corner?

"Grateful" vs. "I Belong"

Let's break it down. "Grateful to be here" energy looks like "I hope they think I'm good enough." "I don't want to seem pushy." "I should just be quiet and work hard." "At least I have a job / seat / invite."

"I belong here" energy looks like "God didn't bring me here by accident." "I can add value to this space." "My perspective matters." "If this room can't handle all of me, it's not my final room anyway." You have to understand that belonging does not mean arrogance. It means agreement with the truth that, you are not a diversity favor, you are not an experiment, you are not "one of the good ones" they let in on trial. You are an answer to a problem they might not even know they have yet. You better know this; the room is lucky to have you just as much as you're blessed to be there!

What God Says About Your Place In The Room

Sometimes we talk like God barely squeezed us in. But the Word talks differently "Your gift will make room for you." "You are seated in heavenly places." "You are His workmanship, created for good works He prepared in advance." That means, there are rooms you're assigned to, not just rooms you accidentally slipped into. There are tables you're supposed to speak at, not just serve at. There are spaces where your voice is part of God's solution. When you move like "I'm just happy to be here," you move like, you snuck in the back. When you move like, "I belong here," you move like, God walked you through the front door with His hand on your back. Belonging is not about human approval. It's about divine placement.

Signs You're Still In "Guest Mode"

Let's have a *Check yourself* moment. Do you constantly second guess whether you should speak? Do you downplay your wins—"It wasn't a big deal." Do you over-explain or apologize before sharing an idea? Do you avoid asking questions like, "What is the pay range" or "What's the growth plan for this role" because you don't want to rock the boat? Do you feel like you have to prove you're not "like other Black women" to be accepted? If you answered yes to any of these questions, that's what I call being in *Guest Mode*, acting like you're in someone else's house, and trying not to leave footprints. **HER** doesn't walk like a permanent guest. She walks like, a contributor, a co-creator, a daughter of God on divine assignment.

Stepping Into "I Belong Here"

So how do we move from guest energy to grounded presence? Not by faking ego, but by embodying truth:

1. Own your preparation and your gift. You didn't stumble here. You have:
    - experience,
    - insight,
    - spiritual sensitivity,
    - cultural wisdom,
    - education (formal or lived).Stop calling what you carry "nothing special."

Purpose-led move: Make a list of your strengths, achievements, and contributions. Before big rooms, remind yourself: "I bring clarity / creativity / strategy / peace into spaces."

2. Claim your mental and physical space. In a room:
    - Sit at the table, not always at the far edge against the wall.
    - Uncross your arms, relax your shoulders, lift your chin.
    - Make eye contact. Breathe slowly.

Online:

- Stop starting every email with "Just" and "Sorry to bother."
- Say what you need to say clearly: "I'd like to propose…" "I'd like to request…" You don't have to be loud. You just have to be present.

3. Speak once, even if it's small. You're training your nervous system to see "I can speak and the world doesn't end." Set a goal:
    - "In this meeting/room/class, I will contribute at least once."

It could be:

- a clarifying question,
- a short insight,
- support for another good point ("I want to echo what she said and add...").

4. Challenge your inner narrative. When your mind says:
    - "They're gonna think you're dumb,"

you answer:

- "No, that's old fear. I have a right to learn and contribute."

When it says:

- "You're lucky to even be here,"
- you answer:
- "I'm grateful, but I'm also assigned."

In this season of your life Sis, your self-talk has to grow up to match where God is taking you, you feel me?

HER PRACTICE – *Chapter 7*

From "Grateful To Be Here" To "I Belong Here"

HER Reflection:

1. Name the room. What is one "room" in your life where you currently feel like a guest
    - Workplace / specific meeting
    - Church ministry team

- Business / entrepreneurial space
- Academic setting
- Social circle / community group

Write it down: "The room where I feel most like I'm just lucky to be here is __."

2. Your current story in that room. What do you tell yourself when you're there? Finish a few of these:
    - "I hope they don't notice that I..."
    - "I'm probably the only one who..."
    - "I shouldn't ask for..."
    - "I'm not as _ Like they are."
3. Your receipts. Write at least 10 things that prove you are not there by accident:
    - skills
    - experiences
    - perspectives
    - wins
    - character strengths
    - things you bring that the room needs

Example:

- "I understand our clients in a way others don't."
- "I bring cultural awareness and emotional intelligence."
- "I have solved real problems here before."

4. How would you act if you genuinely believed you belonged? Imagine walking into that room fully grounded. How would

you:

- sit
- speak
- ask questions
- negotiate
- follow up

Write a few sentences, let your future self-speak:

"If I had full 'I belong here' energy, I would…"

HER *Prayer*

"God, thank you for every room you've opened to me. I know there are doors I walk through now that my ancestors only dreamed about. At the same time, you know how small I've sometimes felt in those rooms. You know the times I've shrunk my voice, held back my ideas, and treated myself like a guest in places you sent me to.

Today, I give you my impostor syndrome. I give You the voice that says, 'You're not enough. You don't belong. They made a mistake.' Remind me, that you are the one who orders my steps, - that my presence is not an accident, that my perspective is needed. Help me move from 'I'm just grateful to be here' to 'I am grateful AND I belong here.'

Teach me to walk into rooms with humility and confidence—not to dominate, but not to disappear either. When fear tells me to stay silent, whisper courage. When shame tells me I'm out of place, remind me You are with me. Let me honor You not just by entering the room, but by showing up fully once I'm inside. In Jesus' name, men."

HER Move: This week, we practice belonging in a concrete way.

1. Pick ONE specific room or setting. Write it down:
   - "This week, I will practice 'I belong here' in: __."

2. Set one "Belonging Action." Choose ONE action for that space:

Examples:

In a meeting:

- Share at least one thought, question, or suggestion.

In a class/training:

- Ask one clarifying question without apologizing for it.

In your business:

- Raise your rates to reflect your actual value.

In ministry/community:

- Volunteer your idea for how to improve something, instead of just doing behind-the-scenes work.

3. Use your "I belong here" statement. Before entering that space, say (out loud if you can} Then, take the action you planned—even if your voice shakes, even if it feels small:
   - "God, You and I are walking into this room together."
   - "I am not a guest in my own calling."
   - "I am allowed to be seen and heard here."
   - "I belong in every room You send me into."

4. Debrief with kindness. Afterwards, journal:
    - What did I do differently this time
    - How did my body feel before, during, after
    - What actually happened
    - What didn't happen that my fear said would happen

   Then write one sentence: "This is one way I showed up like I belong: __."

Sis, it's not about becoming loud and flashy. It's about becoming present and rooted. You're not begging for a seat anymore. You're bringing **HER** to the table, healed, evolving, and slowly learning to sit like she was always meant to be there.

CHAPTER 8

SKILL, STRATEGY, AND THE BAG

She stared at the number on the offer letter. It was... fine. Not horrible. Not amazing. Her first thought wasn't, "Is this aligned with my experience and value"? It was, "Well, it's better than what I had. I should just be grateful." A little voice whispered, "You could ask for more." A louder one shouted, "Don't push it. Don't be greedy. They might take it back." So uh, so- she signed. No questions. No counter.

Six months later, she found out a new hire—with less experience—was making more. Her stomach sank. "Why didn't I at least ask"? Sis, if you have been here before, you know, that question has sat heavy on a lot of our chests.

This chapter is about three things your skill – what you really bring to the table, your strategy – how you move on purpose, not just grind aimlessly and the bag – your money, your opportunities, your earning power. Let me say this, **HER** is not just healed and spiritual—she's also strategic.

We've Been Taught To Hustle, Not To Strategize

Let's start here, Black women are not lazy. If anything, we've been doing too much for generations. Working jobs and running households. Serving at church and holding the community together. Being the backbone, the fixer, the one who gets it done. The problem isn't lack of effort. The problem is unfocused effort. We were taught to work twice as hard, keep our head down and don't complain. Unfortunately, we were not always taught, document your wins, negotiate your worth, set a growth plan and position yourself for the next level. Subsequently, we end up, hustling hard, staying loyal, but not always advancing in a way that reflects what we carry.

Sis, this chapter is your gentle reminder: you don't just need grind, you need a game plan, you feel me!

Step 1: Naming Your Skill (For Real)

Before you can ask for more, level up, or build anything, you have to know what's already in your hands. Black women often minimize our skills ("Oh, it's nothing, I just do it"), confuse struggle with skill ("I've just always handled chaos"), forget that what's "easy" for us is not easy for everybody. Let's break your skills into three lanes:

Lane 1- Hard skills (technical / job-related) examples:

- - Project management
- - Writing, speaking, teaching

- - Coding, design, data analysis
- - Nursing, consulting, sales
- - Doing hair, makeup, styling
- - Event planning, logistics

Lane 2 - Soft skills (relational / leadership) examples:

- - Conflict resolution
- - Coaching and mentoring others
- - Emotional intelligence
- - Cross-cultural awareness
- - Public speaking, facilitation

These are highly valuable and often under-acknowledged—especially in Black women who've been holding families and teams together for years.

Lane 3 - Lived-experience wisdom, examples:

- Navigating systems as a Black woman
- Building from scratch with limited resources
- Understanding community needs and culture
- Turning pain into insight and empathy

That's not "just life "that's leadership training the world didn't pay you for. Purpose-led women start by saying, "This is what I actually carry.

Step 2: From Random Grind To Clear Strategy

Hustle says: "Do everything, all the time, for everyone." Strategy says: "Do the right things, at the right time, for the right reasons." Now, Ask yourself: Where am I going? Not just: - "I want more money" but "I want to be in roles where I __." "I want to run a business that __." or "I want my work to impact __." Strategy for your career or business might look like:

- Identifying a target:
- promotion,
- title shift,
- industry change,
- or income level.
- Making a simple plan:
- What skills do I already have
- What gaps do I need to close
- Who's doing what I want to do that I can learn from

Taking aligned steps: a course, a certification, a mentor, a new project, a conversation with your manager. Strategy is not un-spiritual. You can pray and plan, trust God and update your resume, believe - and build. Faith is not an excuse for passivity. It's fuel for intentional action.

Step 3: Making Peace With "The Bag"

Let's talk about the bag—your money, your earning, your financial growth. Many of us have tangled beliefs about money. "Money is the root of all evil." "Rich people are greedy or fake." "Wanting more is ungrateful." "If I charge for this, I'm taking advantage of people." But, the scripture says, "The love of money is the root of all kinds of evil." Money itself is a tool. In the hands of a healed, purpose-led Black woman, money becomes, margin, options, - access, and legacy.

You can love God deeply and negotiate your salary, be generous and stop underpricing your services, be humble and still say, "That number doesn't align with my experience." Sis, the bag is not your master, it's your resource!

Why We Struggle To Ask For More

When it's time to negotiate, raise prices, apply for that stretch role, many Black women freeze. Underneath it, "What if they say no" "What if they think I'm greedy" "What if I'm not actually that good" "What if I ask for more and they take the whole thing away "So we take the first offer, stay underpaid, stay "reasonable" so we're not "too much." But remember, companies expect negotiation, clients expect clarity, the market expects you to know your range. Other people are asking—boldly—without half your receipts. HER learns to say: "This is my value. This is my range. This is what I bring." That's not arrogance. That's accuracy.

Step 4: Documenting Your Receipts

You can't argue for what you don't remember. Start a "*HER Wins" document*. This consists of a running list on your phone, laptop, or journal where you track:

- projects you led,
- problems you solved,
- revenue you influenced,
- people you developed,
- impact you had.

Examples:

- "Improved process that saved the team hours per week."
- "Handled X number of clients with Y satisfaction rate."
- "Led workshop that helped X women shift __."
- "Increased social engagement / sales / attendance by __%."

When it's time for performance reviews, interviews, bio updates, or pricing decisions, you're not guessing—you're reading your own evidence. This is how **HER** stops asking for crumbs and starts negotiating from clarity!

HER PRACTICE - *Chapter 8*
Skill, Strategy, And The Bag

HER Reflection:

1. Skill inventory.

Make three lists with at least 5 items each:

- Hard skills I have:
- Soft skills I have:
- Lived experiences that shaped my wisdom: Don't be humble-fake. Be honest.

2. Where am I going (for real) Finish at least one of these:
   - "In the next 1–3 years, I would love my work life to look like..."
   - "The kind of work I want to be doing more of is..."
   - "If I wasn't scared, I would pursue..."

3. Money story check. You want to take notice any shame, fear, or judgment. Answer honestly:
   - Growing up, I learned that money is...
   - Women who earn a lot are...
   - When I think about charging more or asking for more, I feel...

4. The gap. Where do you feel most out of alignment right now:
   - Pay
   - Position
   - Use of your gifts
   - Write: "One area where I know I'm living under my potential is..."You know what I mean—this is the groundwork.

HER Prayer

"God, thank You for the gifts, skills, and experiences you placed in me. Thank you for every lesson, every job, every opportunity that has shaped who I am today. You also see the places where I've been playing small—working hard, but not always wisely; accepting less than what aligns with what I carry. Today, I bring You, my fear around money, my discomfort with asking for more, my tendency to downplay my value.

Dear God, remind me that, you are my source, not any one job, client, or person. You gave me these gifts for a reason. It honors You when I steward them well. Show me where I've been hustling without strategy. Show me what next step I can take to align my work, my worth, and my wallet with Your purpose for me. Teach me to move with wisdom, not just grind. Teach me to welcome abundance without worshiping it. Teach me to earn, save, give, and build in a way that honors You and blesses others.

Let me see myself as more than an employee, more than a helper— but as a woman of skill, strategy, and impact. In Jesus' name, Amen."

HER Move: We're going to make one practical money/purpose move this week.

1. Start your HER Wins file.
    - Open a note on your phone, doc on your laptop, or page in your journal.

- Title it: HER Wins – [Your Name].
- Write down at least 10 wins from the last 12–24 months:
- big and small
- work, business, ministry, community

This is your evidence. Add to it regularly.

2. Do ONE strategic action. Pick one of these (or create your own):
   - Career move:
   - Update your resume or LinkedIn to reflect your recent wins.
   - Schedule a meeting with your manager to discuss growth and expectations.
   - Reach out to someone doing what you want to do and ask for a 20-minute conversation.
   - Money move:
   - Research the market rate for your role/skills.
   - Raise your prices (even slightly) if you're undercharging.
   - Start a small "HER Fund" savings pot—even if it's $10 a week—for your future moves.
   - Clarity move:
   - Spend 30–60 minutes mapping out what you'd love your work / business to evolve into over the next 2–3 years.
   - Pray over it and ask God, "Show me one step I can take now."

3. 3. Speak over your work.
    - Before you log in, clock in, show up, or send that email, say:
    - "I bring value to every space I step into."
    - "My work is not random; it is part of my assignment."
    - "I am allowed to be well-paid and well-used by God at the same time."

Sis, every time you move with just a little more clarity and courage around your skill, strategy, and bag, you're stepping further into **HER**—a woman whose spirituality and success don't fight each other, they fuel each other!

CHAPTER 9

EMOTIONAL INTELLIGENCE AND SACRED ANGER

She felt the heat rise before she could name it. They cracked that "little joke" again in the meeting. The one about her "being aggressive" when she asked hard questions. Everybody laughed. She forced a smile. On the inside, a fire lit up, in her chest, in her throat, behind her eyes.

Then came the second feeling, almost as strong as the first: shame. "Don't be that girl. Don't be the angry Black woman. Just let it go." So uh, so- she swallowed it. Again. Later, alone, it came out sideways—tears in the car, short temper at home, exhaustion she couldn't explain.

Sis, that's the cost of never letting yourself feel what you feel, you feel me? This chapter is about understanding your emotions (especially anger), honoring them, and learning how to use them as information and power, not weapons or reasons for shame.

The "Angry Black Woman" Shadow

Let's name the stereotype straight up, many you have heard before, if not about yourself, perhaps of other sisters. The world has painted Black women as loud, irrational, aggressive, "too much," or "difficult." Because of that, many of us over-smile when we're hurt, over-explain when we're firm, over-silence when we're mistreated. We're grieving, but we laugh it off. We're furious, but we call it "I'm fine." We're uncomfortable, but we say, "It's not that deep." Why? Because we don't want to give anyone ammunition to label us what the world already decided we are.

The problem is, when you suppress a real emotion long enough, it doesn't disappear—it corrodes.

Emotions Are Messengers, Not Enemies

Emotional intelligence starts with one simple truth. Feelings are data. Not destiny. Emotions are signals on the dashboard, not the whole engine. They tell you something is off, something matters, something needs attention. Let's look at a few. Anger often signals a boundary has been crossed, a value has been violated, something is unfair or unsafe. Sadness often signals a loss, unmet need, grief for what should've been. Fear often signals a perceived danger, risk, a lack of information or trust. Joy signals alignment, delight, presence. Emotional intelligence is not pretending you're okay all the time, only having "positive vibes." It's noticing what you feel, naming it honestly, and deciding what to do with it on purpose. You can't heal what you won't let yourself even name.

Sacred Anger vs. Destructive Rage

Anger itself is not sinful the Bible literally says, "Be angry, and do not sin." Jesus, flipped tables, called out hypocrisy, confronted injustice. That wasn't Him "losing His temper." That was holy anger in action. So, let's differentiate.

Destructive rage explodes on whoever is closest, not always on the real problem, uses words as weapons, shaming, belittling, tearing down, leaves you and others feeling unsafe and regretful.

Sacred anger tells the truth: "This is not okay," is grounded, not out-of-control, is directed at the right thing (the injustice, the disrespect, the system), not just anybody in range, fuels change, not just chaos.

As a Black woman, your anger is often righteous, at racism, at sexism, at exploitation, at being expected to carry more with less support. The goal is not to "never be angry." The goal is to let anger become a guide, a boundary-builder, a justice alarm, not a constant explosion or a swallowed poison.

Why We're Afraid Of Our Own Anger

Many Black women are scared of their own fire because, we've seen uncontrolled rage destroy relationships. We've seen how quickly our firmness gets misread as hostility. We've been punished harder than others for the same emotional expressions. So, we dial ourselves down, talk softer, make ourselves small, go along to get along. Then what happens? The anger turns inward depression, self-hate, burnout, or it leaks out sideways displayed in sarcasm, resentment, or passive-aggressive behavior. Sis, emotional intelligence is learning how to let the fire warm and light the room, not burn the house down, you feel me.

Building Emotional Intelligence: Feel, Name, Choose

Think of emotional intelligence in three simple moves:

1. Feel – Notice what's happening in your body.

Ask:

- Where is this sitting (chest, throat, stomach, jaw)
- What am I feeling right now (one word if you can)

Instead of:

- "I'm fine,"

try:

- "I feel disrespected / hurt / overwhelmed / anxious / dismissed."

2. Name – Be honest with yourself. Even if you can't say it to them yet, say it to you and to God Naming is not complaining—naming is clarity:
   - "That comment made me feel small."

- "I felt invisible in that conversation."
- "I felt taken advantage of."
- "I felt unsafe."

3. Choose – Decide how to respond, not just react. Once you've named it, ask:
    - "What's the wisest next step"
    - "Do I need to rest, release, or respond"

Options:

- Pray / journal / talk to a safe friend first.
- Decide whether to address it now, later, or not at all (some battles are not yours).
- Set or reinforce a boundary.
- Plan a calm conversation instead of a heat-of-the-moment explosion.

Now this is power! not that you never feel, but that you're not dragged by every feeling you have.

Giving Your Emotions A Safe Place To Land

Black women deserve safe spaces to cry ugly, vent unedited, process un-pretty feelings. Safe spaces might be, therapy, a trusted friend, a journal, a support group, or time with God where you don't censor yourself.

When you don't have any of these, you end up holding it all in your body, using your job, kids, partner, or food as emotional punching bags, or numbing, scrolling, drinking, overworking, overeating, over spiritualizing. It's not weakness to need outlets, it's wisdom. Sis, sometimes the most spiritual thing you can do is cry, write, talk, and breathe, instead of pretending you're "blessed and highly favored" while you're breaking inside.

HER PRACTICE - *Chapter 9*

Emotional Intelligence And Sacred Anger

HER Reflection:

1. Your emotional upbringing. Growing up, what did you learn about emotions—especially anger?
    - Were you allowed to be sad or mad
    - Did you see adults explode or shut down
    - What happened when you cried or spoke up

   Write 5–10 sentences about what emotions felt like in your house.

2. Your current pattern. When you get angry now, what do you usually do?
    - Shut down
    - Cry
    - Lash out
    - Over-explain
    - Pretend you're fine

   Write about one recent situation where you felt anger and how you handled it.

3. Your most common feeling. If you had to pick one emotion that shows up most often in your life right now, what would it be?
    - Angry
    - Anxious
    - Numb
    - Sad
    - Tired
    - Hopeful

Take a moment to reflect, answer this question, What do you think that feeling is trying to tell you?

4. What does "sacred anger" look like for you?

5. If your anger wasn't something to be ashamed of, but a sign from God, what might it be pointing at in your life right now? Write freely, no judgment.
    - a boundary is needed,
    - a conversation is overdue,
    - a system is unjust

HER *Prayer*

"God, You see every emotion I carry the anger I swallow, the sadness I hide, the fear I downplay, the joy I sometimes don't even trust. You know where my fire comes from. The times I've been disrespected, silenced, overlooked, and expected to carry more than is fair. I confess that sometimes I've run from my feelings out of fear of what they mean.

I've been afraid to be honest because I didn't want to be labeled, judged, or rejected. Today, I invite you into my emotional life. Teach me to see my feelings as information, not identity. Teach me to honor my anger without letting it control me. Teach me to recognize when a boundary is needed, when a conversation is needed, and when I need to lay it at Your feet.

Heal the places where my emotions have been wounded by trauma, racism, disappointment, and constant pressure to be strong. Show me safe spaces and safe people where I can let my heart exhale. Show me how to respond with wisdom when my fire rises. Let my anger become sacred—fuel for justice, clarity, and protection, not destruction or self-sabotage. Help me feel fully and still be led by Your Spirit. In Jesus' name, Amen."

HER Move: This week, we're going to practice emotional intelligence in real time, and gently.

1. The Feel & Name check-in (once a day).

Once a day, pause and ask yourself:

- "What am I feeling right now—in one word"
- (angry, sad, tired, hopeful, numb, anxious, peaceful, etc.)
- "Where do I feel it in my body"
- (chest, throat, stomach, shoulders, head)

Write it down or say it out loud.

No fixing. Just noticing.

2. Give your anger one safe outlet. If you've been holding a lot, choose ONE of these:

    - Journal dump:

Set a timer for 10 minutes and write exactly what you wish you could say—unfiltered, no grammar, no editing. Then close the journal. You do not have to send it to anyone.

- Prayer out loud: Talk to God like you would talk to your closest friend.
- "God, I am mad about _. It hurt when _. I'm tired of _."
- Movement release: Put on a song that matches your mood and move—walk, stretch, dance, shadowbox the air—let your body help process what your mind's been holding.

3. 3. Plan one courageous, calm response. Think of a recurring situation that makes you quietly angry:

    - a comment,
    - a dynamic,
    - a demand.

Ask: "Is this something I need to address if "yes", write a simple script like:

- "When you make jokes about me being 'too much,' it makes me feel disrespected. I need that to stop."
- "I'm not comfortable being spoken to that way. Let's keep our communication respectful."
- "I feel overwhelmed when I'm given last-minute tasks repeatedly. I need more notice, or I won't be able to take them on."

You may not say it this week—but just writing it is a step toward sacred anger and emotional clarity. Sis, every time you allow yourself to feel, name, and choose instead of stuffing or exploding, you are evolving. HER is not a robot. HER is a whole, emotionally honest, spiritually grounded woman who can carry fire in her chest without burning herself down.

CHAPTER 10

RELATIONSHIPS, COMMUNITY, AND SISTERHOOD

Her phone was full... and she was lonely. Group chats popping. Memes. "Sis!" "Girl!" "Bestie!" Story reactions and heart emojis. But when she really needed somebody—-not for laughs, - not for surface talk, - but for "I'm not okay, can you sit with me in this"— she scrolled through her contacts and hesitated. Thought after thought, hesitation in her mind "I don't want to be a burden." "They've all got their own stuff." "I'm the strong one. I don't know how to be the one who needs." That's a quiet ache a lot of Black women carry. We're surrounded by people but starving for real support. This chapter is about healing how you relate, building community on purpose, and letting sisterhood become part of your rise, not just your hashtag.

The Lie Of "I Don't Need Anybody"

Somewhere along the line, a lot of us picked up this armor "I'm good. I don't need anybody. I got me." On the surface, it sounds strong. Underneath, it's often driven by "I've been let down too many times." "I don't trust people with my full self." "When I needed help before, nobody showed up." So, we become hyper-independent, stop asking, stop expecting, and call it "strength."

But isolation is not God's design, even Jesus had disciples, close friends (Peter, James, John), let me not fail to mention, people He wept with and prayed with. If the Son of God didn't do life alone, you don't have to either.

When Your Strong Friend Cape Gets Heavy

Being "the strong friend" sounds noble, but it has a shadow. You're the one people call at 2am, the one who listens for hours, the one who gives money, advice, prayer, rides, childcare, strategy—But when you are the one breaking, you freeze. The Questions hit in your mind "Who could I even tell this to" "Will they see me differently" "What if they use this against me later?" Plus, people get used to your role. They assume you're always okay. They rarely ask, "And how are YOU, really" So, you play your part, smile, encourage, pour out.

Meanwhile your own cup is cracking. This chapter is your invitation to keep your strength, but allow yourself support, re-learn how to be held as well as holding others.

Healthy Relationships vs. Draining Ones

Let's talk about the difference. Healthy relationships (friend, family, romantic, community) display mutual care, you both give and receive over- time, they display honesty you can tell the truth without walking on eggshells, they display safety, you can share struggle without it being gossip material, lastly, support they celebrate your wins, not compete with them.

In these relationships you often feel, seen, valued, respected, lighter after talking. On the other hand, draining relationships feel like, one-way traffic, you're the therapist, bank, cheerleader, or crisis manager, emotional whiplash, constant drama, unpredictable reactions, smallness you feel like you have to shrink your joy, your boundaries, or your truth. They are guilt traps where love is tied to what you do, not who you are, leaving you often feeling tired, anxious, - used, or "off" in your spirit. Sis, do yourself a favor, check how you feel after you leave a person's presence or hang up the phone—that's the data!

The Wounds That Make Sisterhood Hard

Let's be real: it's not always men or "the world" that hurt us—sometimes it's been other women. The friend who betrayed a secret. The coworker who threw you under the bus. The church sister who judged you instead of helping you. The competition and comparison: hair, body, man, job, calling.

Many Black women carry trust issues, jealousy scars, "mean girl" or "church hurt" memories. So, when we hear "sisterhood," we flinch a little. Nevertheless, we still crave that one (or few) we can call, that group where we don't have to code switch, that circle where we can say, "I'm tired," and they don't demand we explain.

Healing sisterhood doesn't mean pretending the hurt never happened. It means learning to discern, choosing better, and letting God send quality over quantity.

Building Community On Purpose

Real community rarely just "happens. "You build it. Here's how:

1. Be honest about what you need. What do you actually desire:
   - Safe space to vent
   - Prayer partners
   - Business accountability
   - Mom friends
   - Creative collaborators

   Name it: "In this season, I need more __ in my life."

2. Start where you are. Look around:
   - Who already makes you feel more like yourself when you talk to them
   - Who do you leave conversations with feeling seen, not

judged

- Is there one woman you're already a little closer to

Sometimes the beginning of sisterhood is deepening one existing connection, not adding ten new ones.

3. Make small, intentional moves. Examples:
    - Text: "Hey, I really appreciate how you always _. Would you want to grab coffee / a call sometime and catch up for real"
    - Invite one friend over for a low-pressure night: food, sweatpants, real talk.
    - Join (or start) a small group: book club, Bible study, Black women in your field. You don't have to announce, "You are now my official sister." You justshow up,share, see if it's mutual.

4. Pay attention to reciprocity. Early signs:
    - Do they also ask about you
    - Do they follow up
    - Do they respect your boundaries
    - Can they be happy for you

If it's always one-sided:

- you can adjust your level of access without hate,
- love them, but don't make them your inner circle.

Sis, everybody gets love, not everyone gets access, you feel me.

Becoming The Sister, You Also Need

Sisterhood is not just "Who will support me" It's also "Who am I, in other women's lives. Here is an opportunity to "Check yourself." Do you show up only in crisis, or also in joy. Do you listen to reply or listen to understand? Do you hold secrets or pass them in the name of "concern?" Can you celebrate your sister winning in the same area you're still praying for? The healed **HER** doesn't compete, copy, or cling. She cheers, challenges with love, and covers. You are called to be somebody's safe place too!

HER PRACTICE – *Chapter 10*

Relationships, Community, And Sisterhood

HER Reflection:

1. Your current circle. Draw three circles like a target (you can imagine it if you're not drawing):
    - Inner circle: people who really know you
    - Middle circle: people you're cool with, but not deeply vulnerable with
    - Outer circle: associates, coworkers, social media, etc.

   Write a few names in each. Then ask:
    - Who fills me up
    - Who drains me
    - Who am I over-giving to

2. Your story about women. Complete honestly:

- "Women are usually..."
- "Black women friendships are..."
- "I'm most afraid that other women will..." Notice if your beliefs are hopeful, hurt, or guarded.

3. Your longing. If you could have your ideal support system, what would it look like?
   - How many close friends
   - What would you talk about
   - How would you support each other? Finish: "In my dream version of sisterhood, we would..."

4. Your part. Where might you need to grow as a friend/sister this is your honest audit.
   - Do you struggle to be vulnerable
   - Do you disappear when you're going through it
   - Do you struggle with jealousy or comparison

Write: "One way I want to grow in how I show up in sisterhood is..."

HER *Prayer*

"God, thank you for the people you've placed in my life—the ones who've stayed, the ones who were there for a season, and even the ones who taught me what I don't want. You see every wound I carry from relationships gone wrong—friend betrayals, family drama, church hurt, competition, jealousy, and the times I felt alone even in a crowd. Today, I bring you my loneliness, my disappointment, my fear of trusting people again. Heal the places in me that say, 'I don't need anybody,' when really I am just afraid to need. Show me who is safe. Show me who is seasonal. Show me who is covenant.

Dear God, protect me from attaching to people who don't have the capacity to hold what I carry. Grow me into the kind of woman who can be a safe place for others. I ask You for at least one or two real sisters in this season— women I can be honest with, pray with, and grow with. Teach me to build community on purpose. Teach me to receive love without suspicion. Teach me to give love without losing myself. Bless my relationships. Prune what needs to go. Strengthen what needs to stay. In Jesus' name, Amen."

HER Move: This week, we're going to take one small step toward deeper, healthier connection.

1. 1. Reach out with intention. Choose ONE woman:
    - someone you already know but want to know deeper,
    - or someone who has been a quiet blessing to you.

Send a message like:

- "Hey sis, I just wanted to say I really appreciate how you _. I'd love to connect more intentionally—maybe a call or coffee sometime. No pressure, just planting a seed."

or

- "You crossed my mind today and I prayed for you. If you ever want a safe space to talk or just laugh, I'm here." No need to overdo it. Just one genuine reach.

2. Set one relational boundary. Identify one relationship that drains you. Decide one boundary you'll set this week:
    - less time on the phone,
    - not engaging certain topics,
    - not responding immediately to every crisis.

Script example: "Hey, I love you and I care, but I don't have the emotional space for a deep conversation tonight. Can we talk another time / keep it light today" You're allowed to protect your heart.

3. Practice micro-vulnerability. Next time someone asks, "How are you" instead of:
    - "I'm fine," try something a tiny bit truer, with someone who feels at least somewhat safe:
    - "Honestly, I'm a little tired this week, but I'm hanging in there."
    - "I'm grateful, but I've also been feeling kind of overwhelmed."

Sis, you don't have to spill everything. You're just letting yourself feel seen, not just impressive. Trust the process, every time you take a step toward real connection and away from isolation, you're creating a softer landing place for **HER** to evolve and rise, you were never meant to do this journey alone. **HER** heals in community. **HER** evolves in sisterhood. **HER** rises with a tribe.

Part III

RISING

Walking In The Fullness Of Her Power

Chapter 11

MONEY, VALUE, AND NEGOTIATION

The email came through at 3:17 p.m. "Hey, we're excited to offer you..."

She skimmed the numbers. Her chest tightened. It was less than she hoped. Less than she'd quietly prayed for. Less than what she knew some folks around her were making. Her first thought wasn't, "Let's talk." It was, "Don't mess this up. Just take it. Be grateful." Then that now-familiar HER voice whispered:" You teach other women to know their worth. What about you" You know uh, you know-that's the tension right there, fam. The Black woman who can advocate for everybody but herself. This chapter is about healing your money story, standing in your valuc, and learning to negotiate like you actually believe you're HER.

Your Money Story, What Did You Learn Growing Up

Before we talk salary and business numbers, we gotta talk history— what is your personal money script? Reflect back, growing up, what did you see and hear? Maybe it was the statements of: "We don't have it," "Money doesn't grow on trees," "As long as the bills are paid, we're good," "Rich folks are selfish / fake / shady," lastly, "We're not those kind of people."

You might have watched; lights get cut off and then come back on. Do you recall when your mama or grandma stretch meals like they were magicians? I myself can recall from my own childhood of my parents arguing over money behind half-closed doors. We grow into mature adults not realizing the impact of people getting praised for "making it work," but not for making a plan.

A lot of Black women internalized scarcity (there's never enough), survival (just get by), shame (if I don't have it, it's because I'm bad with money), guilt (if I do have it, I'm selfish or "acting brand new"), and then, when we step into new income, careers, businesses and that old script still runs in the background.

Real talk, this is why you can level up and still feel like you're "one bill away" from disaster in your spirit. Often times we live in a perpetual state of reliving the days of our childhood where we internalized lack as what life is supposed to be.

Value vs. Salary

You Are Not Your Paycheck (But It Should Reflect You)

Let's get this straight! Your value is infinite as a human being, created by God. Your salary / rate / fee is one imperfect number in a human system. You are not your job. You are not your bank account. But also, your pay should not consistently insult your skills, experience, and contribution. As Black women, we often overperform, overdeliver, and under-ask.

We say, "I'll just prove myself and they'll notice," "I don't want to seem ungrateful," "It's more than I've ever made before, I shouldn't push it." Meanwhile, folks with less experience, less impact, and less receipts are asking bold and getting it. Honoring your value doesn't mean worshiping money. It means you stop agreeing to numbers that keep you in quiet resentment.

Why Negotiation Feels So Scary

Negotiation is really just a conversation about expectations, numbers, and value. But for many Black women, it feels like "I'm being difficult," "I'm asking for too much," "They'll think I'm greedy or ungrateful," or "They'll pull the offer."

So we accept the first number, don't ask about ranges, don't ask for raises, and don't adjust our prices for years. All while battling often with the voice of fear of the old stories of being punished for speaking up, job trauma, racial and gender bias, lastly, a belief that we're always on "thin ice" professionally. The truth is that the entire system expects negotiation; we're the only ones shamed into silence.

Negotiating As HER: *Mindset Shifts*

Let's role play and have the tough conversation. Before we talk scripts, we talk mindset. Changing your thoughts will change what you believe and how others perceive you. It's about time you show up differently. Remember:

1. You are not begging, you are aligning.
    - You're not on your knees asking for a favor.
    - You're at the table, discussing a fair exchange.
    - Their question: "Can we get your skills, energy, time, and talent for this number"
    - Your question: "Does this number honor what I bring and what this role requires"

2. No is data, not a death sentence.

If they say:

- "We can't move on base salary,"
- that doesn't mean:
- "You were stupid for asking."
- It means:

You now have information:

- about their flexibility,

- about their budget,
- about whether this is the right place.

3. You can negotiate more than money.

Sometimes the bag is:

- base pay,
- bonus,
- vacation,
- remote days,
- title,
- professional development support.

Value is bigger than one line item.

4. In business, your price is not a confession of greed.

Charging:

- sustainable, fair rates

allows you to:

- stay in business,
- serve well,
- not resent your clients.

Undercharging:

- burns you out,
- disrespects your own time,
- often leads to working more while still struggling.

Renewed mindset thinks like: HER rates are not random; they're rooted in math, value, and wisdom. Let's make it plain, it time to walk out your next career move:

Practical Negotiation Moves (Job or Contract)

Step 1: Do your homework. Before you negotiate:

- Research salary ranges for your role / industry / location.
- Look at multiple sources (Glassdoor, salary.com, LinkedIn, people in your field).
- Ask trusted peers for ballparks: "For someone with X years and Y skillset, what's reasonable"

Step 2: Know your non-negotiables. Ask:

- "What's the minimum number I can accept without resentment"
- "What would feel aligned with my experience and responsibilities"
- "What extras matter to me (benefits, schedule, growth)"

Step 3: Calm, clear language.

When they give you a number, instead of just:

- "Okay, sounds good,"

you can say:

For salary:

- "Thank you for the offer. Based on my experience with [X], [Y], and [Z], and my research on market rates for this role, I was expecting something in the range of

[$A–$B]. Is there room to move closer to that"

For business / freelance:

- "For the scope of work you're describing, my rate is [$X]. This reflects the time, expertise, and outcomes I'll be bringing to the project."

If they say no:

- "I understand. Given that, is there flexibility in [vacation, title, signing bonus, remote days, professional development budget]"

Show up for you- you're just asking questions, not cussing anybody out. You owe to yourself to be compensated for the work you do.

Healing The Guilt Around More

Let's talk about that little voice that says, "You're doing too much. Be content," "Look at where you came from. Isn't this enough," "If you make more, what will people say?" Here's the thing contentment is a heart posture, not a wage cap. You can be grateful and still grow. You can remember where you came from and refuse to stay mentally stuck there.

More money in the hands of a healed, purpose-led Black woman means debt paid down, options for your kids, resources for your parents, breathing room for your nervous system, seed money for your business, generosity without self-erasure. You're not chasing money for ego. You're positioning your life for stability, legacy, and service. Sis, I need you to understand that's not greed, that's stewardship!

HER PRACTICE – *Chapter 11*

Money, Value, And Negotiation

HER Reflection:

1. Your money story.

Finish these sentences honestly:

- "Growing up, money was usually a source of…"
- "In my family, people who had money were seen as…"
- "When I think about asking for more money now, I feel…"

2. Where you feel under-valued? Right now, where do you suspect you're being undervalued?

- Salary / hourly pay
- Business pricing
- Side services you do for free
- Emotional labor you do at work

Write: "One place I know I am underpaid / under-compensated / under-acknowledged is…"

3. 3. Your receipts list.

List at least 10 concrete receipts from the last 1–3 years:

- Problems you solved
- Money you helped make or save
- People you led or developed

- Systems you improved
- Outcomes you contributed to
- No modesty here—facts only.

4. 4. Your next money level vision.
   - Finish: "Within the next 12–24 months, I'd like my financial reality to look more like..." (Be specific: income, debt, savings, type of work.) You know what I mean—this is your starting point for real change.

HER *Prayer*

"God, I thank You that You are my Source. Before a paycheck, a client, or a contract, it was always You sustaining me. You also see the fear, shame, and confusion I've carried around money. The times I've settled for less than what was fair. The times I've over-given and under-charged. The times I've felt guilty even wanting more. Today, I bring You my money story, my family patterns, my mistakes, my fears about not having enough, and my fears about having more.

I ask You to renew my mind about money. Teach me to see it as a tool, not a god. Teach me to steward it with wisdom, not fear. Teach me to earn in line with my value and assignment. Give me courage to negotiate where I've been silent. Give me language to advocate for myself without apology. Give me discernment to know when to stay, when to ask, and when to go. I surrender both my scarcity and my striving to You. Lead me into a financial future that honors You, sustains me, and blesses others. I am not chasing riches; I am chasing obedience. But I refuse to believe that obedience must always equal lack. Thank You that as I Heal, Evolve, and Rise, You are also healing my relationship with the bag. In Jesus' name, Amen."

HER Move

This week, we're going to take ONE concrete step toward aligning your money and your value.

1. 1. Do a reality check: your number vs. the market.

   Pick one focus:

    - your job,
    - your main service/business,
    - or your next role.
    - Do 30–45 minutes of research:
    - Look up average salaries / rates.
    - In your city or remote market.
    - For your experience level.

   Write down: "The range I'm seeing for what I do is: __." Compare it to what you're currently making or charging. No judgment—just data.

2. Decide on a "HER number." Based on:

    - your research,
    - your receipts,
    - your responsibilities,

   decide: "A number (salary or rate) that would feel more aligned with my value right now is: __." This might be:

- a raise target,
- a new package price,
- a new hourly/session rate.

3. Take ONE step toward that number. Options:

If you're employed:

- Draft an email requesting a meeting about compensation/growth.
- Outline your receipts in a doc to bring to that conversation.
- If you're not ready to ask yet, set a date within the next 60 days.

If you run a business / side hustle:

- Raise your rate for new clients (even if it's a small bump).
- Create or update one package that reflects your true time and energy.
- Practice saying your new price out loud until it feels less scary.

If you're between jobs:

- Use your new "HER number" to filter roles you apply to.
- Practice your negotiation script out loud.

Script starter: "Based on my background in _ and the market range for this type of role, I'm targeting compensation in the range of _ to __."

The goal isn't to fix your whole money life in one week. It's to start acting like a woman who believes "My work, my time, and my expertise deserve to be honored." That's **HER**.

CHAPTER 12

RISING AT WORK WITHOUT LOSING YOUR SOUL

By the time she pulled into the parking lot, she already felt the shift. In the car Gospel, lo-fi, or quiet—her breath was steady. At her desk, Slack pinging, emails dinging, folks already lined up at her door. "Hey, quick question...", "Can you look at this real quick..." ,"Did you see that new thing leadership wants us to do...",She was good at her job. Too good, maybe.

So good that everybody came to her, everything flowed through her, and her days blurred into a cycle of putting out fires for other people. She'd prayed for a "good job." Now she had it. But somewhere along the way, her peace had gone missing. She thought "If I rise higher in this, will I just get more of this chaos," "How do I grow here without losing myself?"

Sis, if you've ever felt like your job was paying you in direct deposit but draining you in spirit, this chapter is speaking directly to you, lets dive in!

The Reality Of Being A Black Woman At Work

Let's name it plain, work, for a lot of Black women, is a place of opportunity, a place of pressure, and often a place of constant code-switching and calculating. You might be the only Black woman in the room, or one of a few. Daily, navigating coworkers who underestimate you, imitate you, or fear you. Not to mention, balancing hyper-visibility ("They're watching everything I do") and invisibility ("No one sees what I actually do").

On top of all that, you're asked to do emotional labor—educating people, smoothing over tension, being "the calm one," represent "diversity" on panels, photos, or committees, without always being given real power.

Rising in that environment is complicated. You want to advance, but you don't want to become someone you don't recognize. I get you want leadership, but you don't want to trade your soul for a title. This chapter is about that tension.

Your Work Is Not Your Whole Identity

Let's start with a small reminder, your job is something you do, it is not the fullness of who you are. To be honest, we've seen titles change, companies restructure, managers come and go. But, the thing that never changes are your identity as God's daughter, your purpose, and your gifts. Those are bigger than any organization's org chart.

When you forget that, you attach your worth to

performance reviews, which let your boss's mood dictate your self-esteem, subsequently, leaving you to feel like a failure if you're not constantly climbing. Rising at work without losing your soul mean "I care, I show up, I do excellent work—but I do not worship this place."

What "Losing Your Soul" At Work Looks Like

You don't usually lose your soul all at once. It's slow. The subtleness of the signs is what catch you by surprise. Before this becomes you let's look at the signs of your drifting. In the beginning, You ignore your body, always tired, headaches, Sunday dread, but you keep pushing. You ignore your spirit, no prayer, no stillness, no joy—just grind and collapse. If you cant relate to what I have stated so far, perhaps, these will resonate with you, ignoring your values, laughing at things that bother your spirit, tolerating disrespect, participating in stuff that doesn't sit right just to "fit in" or keep the check, ignoring your future self by staying in roles you've clearly outgrown, you find yourself letting fear of change keep you stuck. Rising without your soul just means you moved up floors in a building you don't even want to be in.

Redefining "Rising" For HER

For HER, rising is not just about the promotions, title changes, or salary bumps. Those matter—we just talked money in Chapter 11. But rising also means more alignment with your values, more integrity with your calling, more peace in how you move, and more influence used for good, not ego. Take a moment for a Self-Check and Ask: - "Am I rising in title but shrinking in spirit" or - "Am I rising in a way that feels true to who I am becoming"

Rising HER-style might look like saying no to a role that would pay more but destroy your health. Its pivoting into work that uses more of your real gifts, staying in your job, but working differently with boundaries, clarity, and purpose.

Navigating Workplace Politics Without Becoming Fake

Let's talk politics. This is a big one, and unavoidable in the corporate workplace, every job has power dynamics, unspoken rules, and personalities. You can't pretend that away, but you also don't have to lose your authenticity to navigate it.

Here are some principles to help you navigate your way through:

1. Learn the landscape, but don't let it define you.
    - Pay attention:
    - Who actually makes decisions
    - Who influences them
    - How information moves
    - Where bias might be sitting

Instead of just grinding at your desk:

- build relationships,
- ask questions,
- observe.
- But remember:
- the system is real,
- God is bigger.

2. Document don't just feel.

When it comes to:

- wins,
- incidents,
- microaggressions—

Keep records:

- emails, dates, outcomes.
- your contributions and performance. This:
- protects you,
- supports your requests,
- and gives you clarity when considering staying or leaving.

3. Choose your battles—strategically. You don't have to correct every slight. Ask:
    - "Is addressing this worth my energy right now"
    - "Will speaking up here serve my peace, my values, or others"
    - "Is this a pattern I can't ignore, or a one-off I can release"

Sometimes rising means, standing your ground. Sometimes it means not giving everything your full fire. HER is not controlled by chaos, she's led by purpose.

Protecting Your Soul While You Rise

Here are some anchors:

1. Spiritual rhythm around your work.

Before work:

- a short prayer,
- affirmation,
- or scripture.

Example: "God, go before me. Let my work be worship, not slavery. Guard my mind, my mouth, and my heart."

After work:

- a simple ritual to "close the day":
- short walk,
- music,
- journaling one win and one release. Let your body and mind know "Work is over. I can put it down."

2. Emotional boundaries. You can care about your work without:

- tying your whole mood to every email.
- internalizing every piece of feedback as a personal attack.

When something hard happens:

- pause,
- breathe,
- ask: "Is this about my work, my worth, or their issues"

Often:

- it's about their issues.

3. Professional boundaries, we started this in HEAL, now we apply it here:
    - Decide your latest response time (within reason for your industry).
    - Block out focus time where you're not available for constant "quick questions."
    - Stop being the default fixer for everything outside your role unless it's strategic for you.

4. Exit clarity. Sometimes rising without losing your soul means:
    - exiting.

Not every job is meant to be:

- forever,
- or your final form.

Ask God:

- "Is this a place to stay and grow"
- "Or a place to glean what I need, then go" Leaving is not losing. Sometimes it's the most spiritual move you can make.

HER PRACTICE – *Chapter* 12

Rising At Work Without Losing Your Soul

HER Reflection:

1. Your current work reality.

Be honest:

- "Right now, my job makes me feel mostly: __."
- (drained, challenged, bored, grateful, trapped, hopeful, etc.)
- "When I think about being here 1 year from now, I feel: __."

2. Ways you've been losing pieces of yourself. Where do you feel you've compromised too much?

- Letting disrespect slide
- Overworking constantly
- Saying yes to everything
- Hiding your true self (faith, personality, ideas)

Write: "One way I know I've been losing myself at work is…"

3. Signs of life. Not everything is dark. Where do you feel most alive in your work:

- Certain tasks
- Certain people
- Teaching, leading, creating, problem-solving

Write:

- "When I do __ at work, I feel most like myself."

4. Your definition of rising. For you personally, in this season, how would you define "rising at work" Finish:
    - "Rising at work, for me, looks like..."
    - You know what I mean—this gets you clear on what you're actually aiming for.

HER *Prayer*

"God, thank You for the work You've allowed me to do—the jobs that paid my bills, taught me skills, and carried me through different seasons. You also see the parts of me that have gotten tired, jaded, or small in certain workplaces. The times I've let stress run my life. The times I've let fear of losing a job make me lose myself, you feel me. Today, I surrender my career to You again. I give You: my ambitions, my disappointments, my fear of not having enough, my fear of outgrowing where I am. Show me how to rise without losing my soul.

Teach me to work with excellence, not perfectionism, navigate politics without becoming fake, set boundaries without fear, advocate for myself without shame. If this is a place I'm meant to stay and grow, give me strategy and favor. If this is a place I'm meant to leave, give me clarity, courage, and open doors. Remind me that my title does not define my identity.

I am Your daughter first, always. Guard my heart at work. Guard my mind from anxiety.

Guard my spirit from bitterness. Let my presence at work

be light, not just labor.

In Jesus' name, Amen."

HER Move: This week, we take one small but real step to rise in a way that honors your soul.

1. Choose your focus: Stay, Grow, or Go (for now). Prayerfully ask:
    - "In this season, do I sense I'm meant to:"
    - stay and stabilize,
    - stay and grow,
    - or prepare to go

   Write down which one feels most true right now. (This can change later.)

2. Pick ONE soul-protecting action for work. Based on your focus If you're staying (for now):

   Create one boundary:
    - a stop time,
    - one no per week,
    - one blocked focus hour.

   Add one soul-care moment around work:
    - 5-minute morning prayer,
    - end-of-day reflection,
    - a short walk before going inside at home.

   If you're growing where you are:
    - Schedule a conversation with your manager about:

- goals,
- development,
- opportunities.
- Start your "HER Wins" doc if you haven't.
- Volunteer for one strategic project that aligns with where you want to go.

If you're preparing to go:

- Update your resume / LinkedIn.
- Reach out to one contact about roles or referrals.
- Spend 30 minutes looking at roles that match your new HER standards (title + pay + values).

3. Create a simple "work affirmation" for this season. Example:
    - "My job is not my God. God is my source."
    - "I can rise here without losing who I am."
    - "If this door closes, God has others."
    - "I bring value to my workplace, and I deserve to be respected."

Say it:

- before you log in,
- or when work stress starts climbing your back.

Sis, every time you protect your soul while you pursue success, you're rising the **HER** way.

You're not just climbing ladders; you're climbing in alignment!

Chapter 13

LEADERSHIP: FROM SEAT AT THE TABLE TO OWNING THE ROOM

She was there! Name on the agenda. Chair at the table. Camera on in the Zoom box with "Manager," "Director," "Founder," "Lead" floating under other people's faces. She had the seat she once prayed for. Nonetheless inside, she didn't feel like a leader. She felt like, the glue, the fixer, the translator, the one who made other people's leadership look smooth.

It felt as if other folks spoke with ease. But, when she opened her mouth, she felt like she had to over-explain, do extra to prove she deserved to be there, or soften everything so no one felt threatened. She thought, "Am I actually leading—or am I just sitting here making this table more diverse?" Sis, that's the gap we're closing in this chapter. This is about moving from, "I'm just honored to have a seat" to "God trusted me to shape what happens in this room!"

Leadership Is Not Just Title, It's Presence

Let's strip it down. Leadership is not your job title, your follower count, your mic on stage, or your name on the flyer. Leadership is influence – how your presence shifts things, integrity ,who you are when no one's watching, what is your impact? Is there a change that happens because you are in the picture? Candidly speaking, you can be a supervisor with no real leadership, and a receptionist with tremendous leadership depending on how you move.

A Black woman leading at work, in a business, in church, or in her family is often doing it long before anyone gives her a title. She's the one people go to for wisdom, the one who calms the room, and the one who sees what's actually happening under the surface. If you are honest with yourself, you know that half the time you've been leading and didn't even call it leadership, you just showed up and did!

Why "Seat At The Table" Isn't Enough

For years, we've been told "We just need a seat at the table," and that representation matters, of course it does, but a seat alone can become tokenism, decoration, and performance. A seat without voice, influence, and support is just you sitting front row to decisions you didn't actually help make. I want to be clear when I say owning the room doesn't mean, dominating, talking over people, or being the loudest. It means showing up fully as yourself, using your voice with intention, bringing your perspective and your power to the table. It is not asking, "Do I have a right to say something" but "What is my responsibility to add here?"

The Extra Weight Of Leading As A Black Woman

Leadership hits different when you're a Black woman. You're not just thinking about the work, you're navigating how you are perceived doing it. Have you ever been in those moments where you second guess yourself in fear or how others are perceiving you? If you have ever experienced the internal Questions swirl of "If I'm firm, will they call me harsh," "If I'm direct, will they call me angry," "If I'm soft, will they call me weak", "If I take charge, will they say I'm doing too much"? Look Sis, you might be, younger than some you lead, Black in a mostly non-Black environment, a woman in male-dominated spaces, or the one who broke into rooms no one in your family had been in before.

Trust me, I know, you feel the eyes, you feel the expectations, you feel the pressure to be perfect so no one can say, "See, this is why we don't usually let them..." Hey, you know- I know that's a heavy crown, you feel me? But here's the truth, I need you to know that God did not send you into those spaces to be a mannequin. He sent you as salt and light, not silent and a light-skinned with a diversity hire energy.

HER Leadership is Soft, Strong, Spirit-Led! The world often gives you two extremes, cold, cutthroat leader, or self-sacrificing, martyr mother figure who never says no. HER leadership is different. She is, Soft + Strong! She can be compassionate and clear; she can correct without crushing and she can be kind without being a pushover.

She is Spirit-Led + Strategic a woman who, prays and plans, she trusts God and checks the data, she makes decisions with wisdom, not just vibes. I speaking of a woman who is

Secure + Accountable, she doesn't need to be the star to know she's valuable, a woman who can own her mistakes and take feedback without collapsing. Sis, leadership for HER is not about ego! It's about stewardship—caring for people, projects, and spaces God put in her hands.

From Quiet Seat Warmer To Room Shaper

Let's talk about how you move from "I'm just here." to "I'm here, and I'm bringing something." Hey, it's time to you to show up in a real **HER** way!

1. Prepare like your voice matters.
    - Before key meetings / calls / gatherings:
    - Review what's on the agenda.

Ask yourself:

- "What insight can I bring"
- "What question needs to be asked that no one else is asking"
- "Who is not in this room who will be affected by these decisions"

Jot down:

    - 1–3 points or questions you might raise.
    - You're not just reacting in real time—you're leading on purpose.

2. Speak once on purpose. Not to hear yourself talk. To participate like a leader. It could be to set a simple goal:
    - "In this meeting / room / group, I will contribute at least once."
    - offering a solution,
    - supporting someone else's good idea,
    - asking a clarifying question that moves things forward.
    - Leadership doesn't sit silently in every space and call it humility.

3. Advocate for people who can't speak freely. As a leader, part of owning the room is:
    - making sure others are seen.

Examples:

- "I'd like to hear what [Name] thinks; she's close to this work."
- "I want to give credit to [Name]—that idea started with her."
- "We need to think about how this will affect the team on the ground, not just leadership."
- You use your access to widen the circle, not just secure your own spot.

4. Make decisions that align with your values, not just your fears. Questions to ask yourself:

- "If I wasn't scared, what would I decide here"
- "What choice honors both the mission and the people"
- "Am I making this move from faith or from fear of losing my position"

Sis, **HER** doesn't build a throne on other people's backs, you feel me!

Leadership Beyond The Job

Even if you're not "in management," you're likely leading somewhere, in your household,

in your friend group, in your church, in your business or side hustle, or online in how you influence others. Owning the room there might mean setting vision for your family instead of just surviving days. It may even look like leading your team / clients with clear expectations and boundaries. It may also look like running your ministry or platform with integrity, not just aesthetic. Leadership is not "out there." It's already in your daily life.

The question isn't "Am I a leader "It's "What kind of leader am I becoming?"

HER PRACTICE – *Chapter 13*

Leadership: From Seat At The Table To Owning The Room

HER Reflection:

1. Where are you already leading

List all the spaces where you carry leadership (title or no title):

- At work: __
- In business / projects: __
- In church / community: __
- In your family / relationships: __

Then ask:

- "Where do I most feel like a leader"
- "Where do I least feel like one"

2. Your leadership style. People often think of you as:

- The peacemaker
- The strategist
- The encourager
- The straight-shooter
- The nurturer
- The creative
- The organizer

Circle or write what fits. Then write:

- "One strength I bring to leadership is..."

3. Your leadership fear. What scares you most about fully owning your leadership

Complete:

- "If I really step into my leadership, I'm afraid that..."
- (They'll call me bossy / I'll fail / I'll be alone / I'll be targeted / it'll be too much.)

4. Your leadership vision. Close your eyes and imagine the HER version of you leading well.

- How does she talk
- How does she handle conflict
- How does she treat people under her influence
- How does she use her platform

Write a few sentences starting with:

- "The leader I'm becoming is a woman who..."

You know what I mean—ownership starts in how you see yourself!

HER *Prayer*

"God, I thank You that leadership is not just for a certain type of person. Thank You that You've given me influence, gifts, and spaces to steward. You also know the times I've shrunk back—sat quiet, held back ideas, or downplayed my role—because I didn't want to be judged, labeled, or attacked. Today, I bring You my leadership: the rooms I'm in now, the rooms I desire to be in, and the people who look to me for guidance. Dear God, heal the parts of me that are scared to be seen. Heal the parts of me that think leadership means I have to be perfect. Heal the parts of me that believe I have to lead like someone else to be effective. Teach me to lead like HER, soft and strong, spiritual and strategic, humble and confident.

Help me to use my voice wisely, advocate for those who don't have a seat to make decisions that honor You and honor people. Guard my heart from ego and from fear. Lord

keep me grounded so that as I rise, I don't lose who I am in You. Let every room I enter be better because I brought my full, authentic, God-guided self to the table. In Jesus' name, Amen."

HER *Move*

This week, we're going to practice owning the room in one specific way:

1. Choose ONE leadership space to focus on.

Pick:

- a work meeting,
- a church/team meeting,
- a client call,
- a family discussion,
- or an online space you lead.

Write it down:

- "This week, I will practice HER leadership in: __."

2. Set one clear leadership intention. Examples:
   - "In this meeting, I will share one idea or ask one brave question."
   - "In this family conversation, I will calmly state a boundary or direction instead of just going along."
   - "With my team/client, I will clearly communicate expectations instead of assuming they know." Write your intention as: "As a leader, I will __."
3. Do one visible, intentional leadership act. Ideas:
   - Give credit publicly to someone who deserves it.
   - Speak up to challenge something that doesn't align with your values.
   - Facilitate a conversation, not just sit through it.
   - Make a clear decision you've been avoiding and communicate it respectfully.
   - Even if your voice shakes. Even if your hands are sweating. Do it anyway.
4. Reflect afterward. Journal:
   - What did I do
   - How did it feel
   - What stories came up in my head before/during/after
   - What actually happened (not what my fear predicted)

Finish with: "One thing I'm proud of in how I led this week is..."

You know Sis, every time you show up a little bit more as the leader you already are, the room shifts—sometimes in ways you can't see right away but leave this chapter with this thought, you're not just sitting at tables anymore. You're shaping them. That's **HER!** Not just invited, but influential, not just present, but powerful and not just seated, but owning the room God trusted her with.

Chapter 14

BUILDING LEGACY: HER BEYOND TODAY

She was folding laundry when the thought hit her. Not a deep prayer moment. Not a vision board session. Just... socks, shirts, and that one towel that never quite dries right. Her kid yelled from the other room, "Ma, can you help me with something?" She paused, and this question dropped in her spirit, what am I really passing on besides clean clothes and a memory of I did what I had to do! She thought about her grandmother's hands, always working. her mother's sacrifices, stories, silent tears, and even her own constant hustle. Immediately, another thought came, I don't just want them to say, she worked hard. I want them to say, because of her, I got to live different. Sis, that's legacy talking, you feel me.

Legacy isn't just what they say at your funeral. It's what they live because you once lived. Legacy Is More Than Money (But Money Matters Too). When we hear "legacy," a lot of us think of trust funds, big inheritances, rich families on TV. AND we think, "That's not me. I'm just trying to keep these bills paid! But legacy is deeper and broader than dollar signs. Legacy is values – what you teach with your life, not just your words, mindsets how the people coming after you think about God, themselves, money, love, work. The memories, how they remember feeling around you. Yes, systems are apart of legacy as well, the habits, resources, and structures you leave in place.

Most of us don't realize the legacy opportunities – doors you crack open that stay open for others and all of these things I mentioned is in addition to money, there are other aspects to money as well, such as insurance, savings, property, and investments. But even if your money is still in process, you are already leaving a legacy. The question is, is it intentional or accidental? Sis, **HER** chooses to make it intentional, you feel me.

The Legacy You Inherited (Good And Hard) Before we talk about the legacy you're building, we honor the one you received. Look back, from your people, you might have inherited resilience, faith, work ethic, creativity, and survival skills. But also, silence around pain, poverty mindsets, patterns of staying in harmful relationships, the "we don't talk about that" culture and the fear around money or risk.

Hear me when I say, Legacy is not just the nice stuff. It's understanding the patterns that we pass down generationally. Some you're called to continue (faith, strength, love), some you're called to break (cycles of trauma, lack, and silence), and some you're called to transform into something healthier. You are not just your ancestors' repetition, you're their evolution, you feel me.

You Are Somebody's Turning Point!

Somewhere in your line, there is a pivot person the first to leave a toxic situation, the first to graduate high school or college, the first to start a business, the first to go to therapy, the first to say, "This ends with me." Guess what, It might be you! That doesn't mean you carry everything alone. What it means is you have the courage to do something different, so those who come after you don't have to fight all the same battles. Let's talk about what that can look like. It can look like, teaching your kids emotional language you never had, handling conflict in ways that don't destroy people, choosing partners differently, talking openly about money, goals, and mistakes, or leaving written prayers, letters, or stories behind. The turning point doesn't look the same for everyone. Nevertheless, the next generations might not know your whole story, but they'll live inside of your decisions, you feel me.

Legacy In Three Lanes: Personal, Family, Community

Let's make this practical and take personal responsibility for the kind of Legacy you are creating starting with your **Personal Legacy** is the HER you leave on the page of time, who you are becoming, it's the story you'll leave behind as a woman. Ask yourself, "If someone told my story in 3–5 sentences, what would I want them to say?" The one thing you do not leave a legacy is "She never stopped working," only. But you want it to be known that "She grew. She healed. She changed. She listened. She loved." Your personal legacy might include your journals, your book (hello), your creative work, your business or ministry, your daily choices to be honest, kind, and brave.

What about your **Family Legacy**, what flows through your bloodline? This can include faith, do you introduce God as a punisher... or a loving Father, or Emotional patterns, is it always "we don't talk about that" or "we can heal from that." Lastly, money, do you pass on only debt and stress, or at least some tools and transparency about money management? It could look like starting a small savings or investment for your kids / nieces / nephews. I was once told that if you cannot save money that the seed of success is not within you! We have a Her obligation to make sure that our financial matters are in order, making a will so your people aren't left guessing if something happens. Finally, having real conversations about mental health, not just, "Pray it away." We have to check in with our loved ones.

How you impact others outside of your family is in building and supporting others, **Community Legacy** talking about your impact beyond your four walls, this is the girls and women you pour into, the neighborhood or online community you serve, the systems you challenge or change. For some It might look like mentoring younger women, creating programs or resources, volunteering your expertise, starting something that outlives your direct involvement. Legacy here isn't about being famous. It's about being faithful to the space God gave you.

Legacy Without Martyrdom

Legacy without martyrdom does not mean you have to die empty, exhausted, and used up, or that you have to always be "on" for other people where you can never enjoy what you're building. In fact, joy, rest, and boundaries are part of the legacy. If your kids, spiritual daughters, or mentees only ever see you tired, bitter, resentful, and overextended, what they may learn is in order to make a difference, I must disappear and

that's not the legacy we're leaving. HER legacy says I built, I loved, I served—but I also laughed, rested, received, and lived. Sis, you're not just leaving them principles, you're leaving them a blueprint for a whole, not hollow, life, you feel me.

Small Legacy Moves That Matter

You don't need a million dollars or a huge platform to start building intentional legacy. It's the simple things that matter such as - Recording voice notes or videos with your stories, Writing letters to your children or future grandchildren, even, saving $25 a month consistently in a "future HER" account.

No one knows when they are going to transition to eternal life, why not make sure you are not leaving a financial burden legacy. Change the **Family Legacy** by getting life insurance so your passing doesn't become a financial crisis. Teaching younger women what nobody taught you by sharing resources: books, budgets, and/or healing tools. Legacy is often built in consistent, quiet moves, not just big dramatic moments.

HER PRACTICE - *Chapter* 14

Building Legacy: HER *Beyond Today*

HER Reflection:

1. The legacy you received. Answer honestly:
    - "From my family / lineage, I inherited these strengths:" (e.g., faith, toughness, humor, creativity, grind)
    - "I also inherited these hard patterns or mindsets:" (e.g., silence, fear around money, unhealthy relationship She was folding laundry when the thought hit her.

2. The legacy you want to leave. Imagine someone you love (child, niece, spiritual daughter, community girl) standing in front of you, years from now. She says:
    - "Because of you, I learned to…"
    - "Because of you, I believed I could…"
    - "Because of you, I didn't have to…"

Write 3–5 of those sentences.

3. Your current impact. Right now, whether you mean to or not, people are already learning from you. Finish:
    - "People who watch my life right now are learning that:"
    - About work: __

- About love: __
- About God: __
- About being a Black woman: __

What do you want to keep communicating, and what do you want to shift

4. One cycle to break, one thing to build.
   - "A cycle I want to break in my family line is..."
   - "Something new I want to start in my family line is..."

You know what I mean—this is where intention starts.

HER *Prayer*

"God, I thank You for the women and men who came before me—for every sacrifice, every prayer, every step they took that made my steps possible. You also see the patterns, the pain, the silence, the lack, and the fears that were passed down along with the strength. Today, I stand in the middle—between what was and what will be. I ask You to help me honor the good I've inherited, heal the harm I've inherited, and partner with You to build something better for those coming after me. Show me the difference between what I'm called to carry and what I'm called to break. Give me wisdom to make choices that my grandchildren and spiritual descendants will benefit from, even if they never know my name. Bless the work of my hands, the words from my mouth, the wealth I build, and the wisdom I share, so that my life becomes a bridge, not a barrier.

Protect me from trying to be a savior—that's Your job. Strengthen me to be a willing vessel who says yes to building with You. Let my legacy be healing, truth, faith, courage, and love. In Jesus' name, Amen."

HER *Move*

This week, we're going to make one intentional legacy move—small but real.

1. Choose your lane for this season. Which area do you feel most drawn to start with right now:
    - Personal (your growth, your story)
    - Family (kids, nieces/nephews, parents, partner)
    - Community (younger women, church, neighborhood, online)

Write: "Right now, I feel led to focus on: __ legacy."

2. Do ONE practical act that future HER will thank you for. Ideas (pick one):

Personal:

- Write a letter to your future self (or future granddaughter) about what you're learning now.
- Start or update a journal where you tell the truth about your journey with God, work, love, and healing.
- Record a 5–10-minute voice note with your story or testimony and save it.

Family:

- Start a small automatic transfer (even $20/month) into a savings/investment account labeled "Legacy / Future Family."
- Initiate one honest conversation with a child/teen/niece about identity, emotions, or faith that you never got.
- Look up basic info on wills / life insurance if you don't have anything in place and write down one action step.

Community:

- Reach out to one younger woman and offer a listening ear or light mentorship.
- Share one resource (book, budget template, therapist info, scholarship, job lead) with someone who could benefit.
- Volunteer once this month in a space that aligns with your heart (youth, women, justice, healing).

3. Name your legacy confession. Write and speak a simple statement:
    - "I am not just surviving my life; I am building a legacy."
    - "The cycles that end with me will free those who come after me."
    - "I am creating a different normal for the women and children connected to me."

Say it when you feel small, behind, or like your work doesn't matter. Sis, legacy isn't only built in big public moments; it's being built right now, in your healing, your evolving, your rising, you feel me. You are HER beyond today a woman whose life will echo in bodies, in bank accounts, in beliefs, long after this chapter ends.

Chapter 15

HER EVERYDAY RISE: LIVING AS HER, NOT JUST READING ABOUT HER

The book was open on her nightstand. Highlighter marks, folded pages, sticky notes with "YES!" and "Ouch" scribbled in the margins. She'd cried in some chapters, nodded hard in others, screenshotted a few lines to send to her girls.

But on a random Tuesday, running late, juggling work, kids, family, and a half-drunk cup of coffee, she caught a thought: "How do I actually live this when life is life-ing, and I don't have 2 hours to be deep every day", You know that's the real question, Sis, you feel me? This last chapter is not about more information. It's about integration, how does HER, begin Healing, Evolving, and Rising in the real rhythm of your everyday life—not just in the moments when you're reading a book or sitting in a session.

HER Is Not A Mood, It's A *Lifestyle*

We're not building a weekend high, a conference buzz, a "that book was good, now back to my regularly scheduled burnout" moment. We're building a way of being. HER is - how you talk to yourself, how you set your calendar, how you make decisions, how you rest, and how you show up. I know some days you'll feel like a whole healed, evolving, rising queen. Then there will be other days, where you might feel like the same old you, just tired with better language. Sis, both days count. Let me say this, you know- HER isn't perfection; HER is direction, you feel me.

The HER Filter: Heal · Evolve · Rise In Real Time

One simple way to carry this into your everyday is to make HER a filter for your choices. In any given situation, you can ask "What would it look like to Heal here," "What would it look like to Evolve here," "What would it look like to Rise here." So let's have the reality of what the tough self-reflective conversations will be after the benediction as the church folks say! A tough conversation in Healing begins with truth and it looks like acknowledging your real feelings. Don't live a lie, notice old triggers coming up and decide not to lie to yourself about what hurts. EVOLVING is the process of prioritizing choosing honest words over fake peace and owning how you show up to protect your peace by using "I feel" language instead of attacking then being intentional to set or reaffirm a boundary. RISING shows up when you have the conversation instead of ghosting, Stand on your worth and make a decision that honors your future, not just your fear. Let's take a look at how your filter responds in real time example for *A work Opportunity*:

HEALING:

- Notice if "I'm not good enough" or "I'm just lucky" stories show up.
- Talk back to them with truth.

EVOLVING:

- Ask clear questions.
- Get the information you need.
- Decide what support or development you'll need.

RISISING:

- Apply.
- Pitch yourself.
- Negotiate.

Sis, you know- you don't have to do all three perfectly every time. But **HER** is always asking, "Where is the healing, evolving, or rising in this for me," you feel me. Designing Your HER Rhythm (Not A Perfect Routine). Let's talk daily life. You don't need a 4-hour morning routine with candles, green juice, and a choir in the background. Look, all you need is anchored touchpoints that keep you from slipping all the way back into autopilot.

Think of it like this: rhythms/routines are just one small HEAL touch, one small EVOLVE touch, and one small RISE touch built into your days or weeks. Let's refer to them as your **HER Check-in:**

HEAL – Soul Check-Ins

Simple ideas:

- 5 minutes in the morning or night to ask:
- "What am I feeling"
- "Where am I hurting"
- "What do I need from God today"
- A weekly journal dump to tell the truth without editing.
- A therapy session, support group, or trusted friend call you keep on your calendar like any other appointment.

EVOLVE – Mindset & Habits Check-Ins

- Saying no at least once a week, where old you would've said yes.
- Practicing one new money habit (budget, saving, tracking).
- Speaking up once in a room you'd usually stay silent in.
- Setting time blocks for work and time blocks for rest.

RISE – Bold Steps Check-Ins, Even If They're Small

- One action a week that stretches you:
- applying, pitching, following up, raising rates, having that conversation.
- Writing and revisiting your vision for where you're headed.
- Checking your choices against:
- "Does this move me closer to the life I'm called to live"

HER is built in inches, not just major leaps, you feel me. There is grace for the slips and setbacks. Let's be real you will not walk this out perfectly, you will say yes when you wish you'd said no. You will go back to an old pattern in a moment of fear or fatigue. You will forget what you wrote in this book on some days and default to survival. Listen, that does not mean you're a fraud, it didn't work, or you're "back to square one." No, sis, progress is not a straight line. It's more like a spiral—you pass similar places, but from a higher level of awareness every time. So, promise the HER in you that when you catch yourself slipping you will pause, breathe, and ask, "What part of me made this choice—Hurt me, or HER me" and - "What can I do differently next time," then forgive yourself, repair what you can, and step forward again. Sis, shame keeps you stuck but grace keeps you moving, you feel me.

Growing HER In Community

You were never supposed to carry all this alone. We talked about sisterhood already, but for the everyday rise, it really helps to have one or two women you can walk this out with. That might look like a monthly HER check-in call:

- "What did you Heal, what did you Evolve, how did you Rise this month"
- reading this together and journaling as a group.
- holding each other accountable on:
- boundaries,

- money moves,
- career steps,
- self-care,
- rest.

Rising is easier when someone is clapping for the versions of you they can't see yet. You know **HER** is personal, but she's not isolated, you feel me. As long as you have breath in your body you will find yourself **Becoming HER Again And Again!** Here's the quiet truth, you've met HER before, yes, it was In the moments you walked away from what was killing you, in the times you spoke up when your voice shook, in that one season you chose therapy, rest, prayer, or a new path and in that decision to forgive, or to press charges, or to leave, or to stay and rebuild with boundaries.

This book didn't create **HER** from scratch. It just helped you to name her, see her, and remember her. Sis, going forward, living as HER will look like, catching yourself sooner when you shrink, coming back kinder when you fall, and trusting God deeper in the in-between. Trust me when I say this, there'll be seasons where you're focused on HEALING more, seasons where you're heavy on EVOLVING, and seasons where RISING is the loudest but all three will always be in the mix. HER is a life-long journey—not a 15-chapter finish line, you feel me. We are on a journey!

HER PRACTICE - *Chapter 15*

Her Everyday Rise: Living As HER, Not Just Reading About HER

HER Reflection:

1. Where am I the strongest right now: Heal, Evolve, or Rise, Circle or choose:
    - HEAL – I've been doing a lot of inner work.
    - EVOLVE – I've been changing habits and mindsets.
    - RISE – I've been taking bold, outward steps.

   Then answer:
    - "In this season, I feel most focused on: __ because…"

2. Where do I feel behind or stuck Circle or choose:
    - HEAL – still avoiding certain wounds or truths.
    - EVOLVE – still stuck in old patterns.
    - RISE – still scared to make visible moves.

   Write: "One area I still feel behind in is…"
    - "If I'm honest, what's been holding me back is…"

3. The HER I'm becoming (1-year vision): Close your eyes and picture yourself one year from now, living as HER day to day. Write a few sentences starting with:
    - "One year from now, as HER, I…"

      (How do you think, move, speak, work, love, rest)

4. Three small anchors for my everyday HER life. Write:
    - "A HEAL habit I will keep: __"
    - "An EVOLVE habit I will keep: __"
    - "A RISE habit I will keep: __"

You know what I mean—these reflections become your personal HER blueprint.

HER Prayer

"God, thank You for walking with me through this whole journey—for every chapter, every mirror moment, every conviction, every comfort. You know uh, you know- You see the woman I was when I opened this book, and You see the woman I am becoming now that I've reached this page, you feel me. I confess that I will not do this perfectly. There will be days I forget, days I fall back into old patterns, days I feel more like the 'old me' than HER. But I also believe that You finish what You start, that Your grace is enough for my process, that I am not walking alone. Lord, help me to keep healing—with honesty and compassion for myself, keep evolving—with courage to change mindsets and habits, keep rising—with boldness to take the steps You place in front of me. Surround me with the right people. Help me to be the right person for others. Guide my work, my money, my relationships, my rest, and my decisions. When I forget who I am, remind me. When I get tired, strengthen me. When I get scared, hold me. Thank You that HER is not a fantasy version of me. HER is the truest version of me—the one You always saw. I commit to living, not just reading, this journey.

Day by day. Step by step. In Jesus' name, Amen."

HER Move: This is your last chapter, but not your last step. Let's seal it with something simple and real.

1. Create your HER Declaration.

Write a short declaration (3–5 lines) you can come back to whenever you feel lost.

Example:

- "I am HER.
- I am healing from what tried to break me.
- I am evolving into who God always knew I could be.
- I am rising—not just for me, but for those connected to me."

Or:

- "I am no longer living just to survive.
- I am allowed to be whole, wealthy, loved, rested, and powerful.
- I walk as HER: healed, evolving, and rising."

Write yours. Keep it where you can see it:

- mirror,
- phone lock screen,
- journal,
- altar space.

2. Choose one 30-day HER focus.

Ask:

- "For the next 30 days, where do I most need to focus: HEAL, EVOLVE, or RISE"

Whichever you pick:

- HEAL – commit to one healing practice daily or weekly (journal, therapy, prayer walks, processing).
- EVOLVE – commit to one habit/boundary shift (saying no, money tracking, screen limits, sleep).
- RISE – commit to one bold action per week (applications, pitches, conversations, raising prices, setting dates).

Write: "For the next 30 days, I will focus on _ and my key practice will be _."

3. Tell someone, share with:
    - a friend,
    - a mentor,
    - a sister,
    - or your community:
    - "I just finished this: HER journey. Here's one thing I'm committed to doing next…"

Let somebody witness your commitment and, if they're safe, ask them to check in. Sis sometimes the difference between a moment and a movement is just one person knowing you're serious, you feel me. As you close this book, remember—you are not behind, broken beyond repair, or too late. You are HER: Healing, Evolving, Rising, again, and again, and again!

Conclusion

I AM HER

HER Was In You The Whole Time

Maybe you started this book tired. Tired in your body. Tired in your mind. Tired in your spirit from being "the strong one" for everybody and barely held by anybody. Maybe you picked it up because something in you whispered "I can't keep living like this. There has to be more than surviving." And now here you are—at the end of these pages, but not at the end of your becoming. If you remember nothing else from this book, remember this, **HER** was never somewhere out there. **HER** was in you the whole time.

Every chapter, every exercise, every prayer was not about turning you into a brand-new person. It was about:- recovering the woman God already saw, clearing out the lies that buried her, loosening the chains that confined her, and giving language to the power you kept trying to hide. You didn't get "given" HER. You remembered HER, you feel me.

You Did More Than Read

Sis, you told the truth about the weight you've been carrying, looked at old stories in your head and dared to rewrite them, unlearned survival that kept you alive but was slowly killing your joy, stared your reflection in the face and chose compassion over constant critique and began to practice boundaries that respect your spirit. Not only that, but you also started shifting from people-pleasing to purpose-led living, dared to believe you belong in rooms you once tiptoed through, started to see your skills, your strategy, and your bag as holy stewardship. Sis, you went deep, you let yourself feel emotions you'd buried under "I'm fine." And opened your heart, even a little, to real community and sisterhood.

Lastly, you began to untangle your money from shame and fear, stood a little taller at work, with your soul still intact, acknowledged that you are a leader, title or not. Mindset changed, you started thinking about legacy on purpose, not by accident, designed tiny, powerful ways to live as HER on regular days, not just special ones. Listen, you are celebrated in this moment, That's not light work! That's holy work!

The World Needs HER

I need you to understand something, your healing is not selfish. Your rising is not a threat to anyone who was truly meant to walk with you, and your evolution is not an insult to where you came from. There are people tied to your obedience. A young girl is watching how you handle your boundaries. A coworker is watching how you carry your faith without losing your edge. A daughter, niece, or neighbor is watching how you talk about your body, your money, your dreams.

I need you to understand that ther is a woman you haven't even met yet who is waiting for the book, the business, the program, the prayer, the hug, the yes that only YOU can bring. Sis, when you Heal, Evolve, and Rise, it doesn't just free you. It sends a quiet permission slip into the atmosphere that "We don't have to live at war with ourselves anymore and we're allowed to be whole." I know the world has been very loud about what Black women should be. **HER** is your answer back, you feel me.

You Are Not Behind

Let me say it again for the version of you that still feels late, you are not behind, not behind in purpose, not behind in healing, not behind in success and not behind in love. Every detour, every delay, every "I thought I'd be further by now" is seen by a God who operates outside of our timelines. You did not miss your only chance. If you're breathing, there is still more.

This is not the end of your story. This is the part in the movie where the main character realizes who she really is. Listen! From here on, when the old voices creep back in—

the ones that say:

- "You're too much."
- "You're not enough."
- "You should have settled."
- "You're asking for too much."
- "Who do you think you are"

I pray something in you rises up and answers, "I am HER, I am allowed to heal, I am allowed to grow, and I am allowed to rise."

A Future With HER At The Center

Imagine with me for a moment, waking up and choosing your day, not just reacting to everyone else's emergencies. Going to work knowing your value and refusing to shrink it or managing your money like a woman who plans to leave something behind besides stress.

This is your time to embrace the seasons of resting without guilt, loving without losing yourself, praying honest prayers, not just polished ones, Laughing more, even if everything isn't fixed yet! Sis, this is not fantasy! This is the life you are already stepping into—step by step, boundary by boundary, decision by decision.

You are building a different normal in your family, a different narrative in your lineage, a different model of what a strong Black woman can be, soft and fierce, spiritual and strategic, generous and boundaried, ultimately, successful and surrendered. You know- HER is not out of reach anymore. She's your everyday option, you feel me.

One Last Blessing, as you close this book, I speak this over you:

- May you never forget your own worth again to make someone else comfortable.
- May you never again call yourself names God never called you.
- May you never again treat exhaustion like a badge of honor.
- May you never again confuse toxicity with loyalty.
- May you never again build everyone else's dreams and bury your own.

May you:

- Heal from what tried to break you,
- Evolve into who God always knew you were,
- Rise into rooms, roles, and realities that match the truth of your calling.

May your daughters—born or spiritual—never have to start as far behind as you did.

May your name be whispered with gratitude by people who never even met you face to face, because your obedience shifted something in the atmosphere. And may you remember, on the days you forget: You are HER. Not someday. Not when you're perfect. Now! In process! In progress! And in God's hands!

Close this book when you're ready. But don't close this chapter in your life.

Heal.

Evolve.

Rise.

Then do it again tomorrow.

Made in the USA
Coppell, TX
11 February 2026